WESTERN CHANGE

WESTERN CHANGE

Summer Saturdays in the West
1957-1995

by

Paul Chancellor

THE RAILWAY CORRESPONDENCE AND TRAVEL SOCIETY

ISBN 090 1115 789

Published by the Railway Correspondence and Travel Society,
11 Suffield Close, Long Stratton, Norfolk, NR15 2JL

COVER DESIGN BY JOHN HOLROYD

Printed by the Amadeus Press Ltd., Huddersfield
Typesetting by Highlight Type Bureau Ltd, Bradford

WESTON-SUPER-MARE: Freight trains normally bypassed Weston on their journeys South using the "main line" direct from Worle-Uphill Junctions. However on occasions it was necessary to overtake a freight and then the freight was "looped" and passed through Weston. This view shows the station looking North and other than the arrival of BR enamel signs it was little changed from pre-war years. In the background can be seen two DMUs in the bay platform. the engine is 5098 *Clifford Castle*. 27th June 1962.

(Michael Mensing)

CONTENTS

TABLES

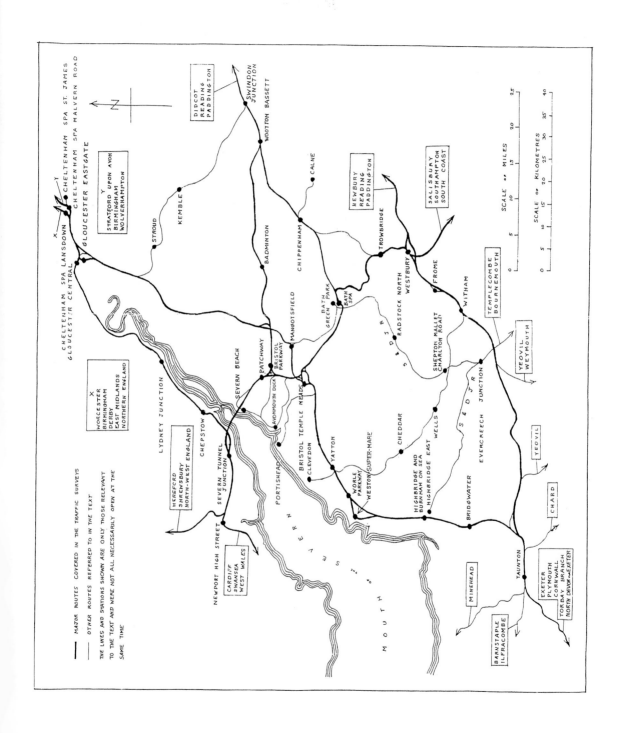

1. Foreword

During the 1960s the Western Region of British Railways was transformed by the replacement of its long serving fleet of steam locomotives with a much smaller number of highly sophisticated diesels.

Using traffic surveys and visit notes compiled by a small group of enthusiasts living in the area the move to diesel traction is charted in this book. The period covered deals mostly with the changes brought about by the introduction of the diesel hydraulic classes, in an area bounded by Taunton, Severn Tunnel Junction, Gloucester and Swindon. The enthusiast can however, using the traffic surveys, also reconstruct a day of main line movements at, for example Reading, see how Somerset and Dorset line traffic fitted in, study the decline of LMS steam on the Bristol-Birmingham route or even pay a brief visit to Exeter Central.

The story would not be complete without mention of the diesel electrics which, in a short period, consigned the hydraulics to the scrap heap, many after less than ten years' work and even *their* demise can be seen with a brief look at the HST and Sprinter dominated services of the 1990s.

The author would like to thank the original team of Stacey Sutton, Bill Bird and Michael Selby as well as those who have contributed contemporary information, and in particular Bill Brooksbank, Russell Leitch and Peter Hall. The maps were prepared by Bill Batteson.

Extracts from "SUMMER SATURDAYS IN THE WEST" (David & Charles, 1973) are by the kind permission of the publishers.

Paul Chancellor
Bromsgrove
May 1995

2. How it used to be

It was a warm summer's day in 1957. The eager boy arrived at Weston-super-Mare station in a Tilling green half cab bus and alighted carrying the obligatory duffel bag containing a packet of sandwiches which were soon to be squashed into some strange shape by the large bottle of Tizer also contained in the bag. The bag would also hold a notebook, a range of pens and of course the appropriate Ian Allan ABC. If particularly affluent this might have become a 'Combined Volume' or a Locoshed Book and in later years the 'Loco Shed Directory' would also be part of the kit.

Entering the ticket office the smell of smoke was strong from years of permeating into the wooden floorboards. The bottom half of the wood panelled room was painted brown, the top half cream – well it used to be cream but it had been a long time since it had seen the paint brush! The ticket clerk peered out from behind his small window set in one wall.

"Cheap day return to Temple Meads please," said the youth handing over half a crown (12$^{1}/_{2}$p). In return a ticket was given which was immediately presented to the ticket collector on the gate. "Oh Dear" – it was the grumpy fat red-faced one again who really didn't seem to care if you travelled or not.

Despite having watched the youth buy the ticket the collector examined front and back and then clipped the appropriate half.

Once on the platform there was time to spare before the train for Bristol was due. This was just as well as there was much to do. Out with the notebook and ABC. Hopefully the Tizer had not yet leaked out of the bottle. A trial with the pens produced the usual crop of those that did not work.

A train occupied the down platform and a walk to the end of the platform would reveal perhaps an unkept Castle which could be met with the well known refrain of 'scrap it' or if it was going to be a good day the number would go into the notebook for action later.

Of more interest was a walk to the Bristol end of the platform as there would always be at least one engine on the turntable line and sometimes three or four would be present. Over the years this could produce anything

from a pannier tank to a visiting Royal Scot or B1. As ever hidden down beside the one road engine shed adjacent to Locking Road station (used mainly for summer excursion traffic) was a very interesting looking engine which was just too far off to get the number. A spotty individual who had set up shop on a trolley near the platform end told the youth it was a rare Hall from Goodwick (whose engines never ventured east of Swansea!) and he was tempted to believe it was true.

The clatter of a signal arm dropping disturbed the peace. This suggested to those in the know that the Bristol train had just passed Uphill Junction some three to four minutes away. Walking back down the platform the youth anticipated what would be on the train – Castle, Hall, Grange – or even a King? Well not on this train, being a semi-fast from Taunton to Bristol. This was more likely to be a 53XX 2-6-0 with three or four coaches.

Jumping aboard it was relatively easy to find a compartment that was empty. Little had changed in terms of provision of services and length of trains in recent years but travellers were finding new ways of getting around especially on the shorter journeys.

The usual routine was followed – drop the opening window in the door, secure by the leather strap if not broken, study the photographs of exotic distant destinations, fall into the seat by the window and sneeze two or three times as the dust rose all around!

Expectancy turned to frustration as the minutes ticked by with no sign of a departure – looking out of the window the reason was plain to see as basket upon basket of produce was loaded into the guard's van. Eventually all doors were closed, the guard blew his whistle, waved his flag and climbed aboard. The engine responded with a toot and the train set off.

A rapid pace is set but soon the brakes come on for a stop at Weston Milton Halt after only some 1$^{1}/_{2}$ miles. As this is not the 'rush hour' only a handful of passengers join and the train is soon underway again. It is only a short run to Worle Junction where the main line from the South West is rejoined, Weston being on a loop line. A long freight train is observed waiting on the main line to follow us to Bristol. Puxton and Worle station is passed within a further two miles. A couple of southbound trains rush by. The young spotter had been hanging out of the window attempting to get the number of the approaching locomotive but with the large reporting numbers used by the Western Region this is rarely possible on express passenger trains. Before reaching Yatton more freights are observed headed by a 28XX or Hall in the loop lines.

Other than the expresses which bypass Weston nearly every passenger train stops at Yatton as it is an interchange station for both the Clevedon and Cheddar Valley lines.

A 14XX with auto coach stands in the Clevedon bay whilst a pannier tank or 45XX could well be at the head of the Cheddar Valley line train. The large assortment of trolleys on the platform are piled high with boxes and baskets being transferred from one train to another.

Once underway from Yatton we will stop only at Nailsea and Backwell before passing through Flax Bourton, Bedminster and Parsons Street non stop. For the spotter there is work ahead, firstly with more passing trains and looped freights and then as Bristol is approached excitement mounts with many numbers to note in the freight yards of Bristol West Depot and the carriage sidings of Malago Vale.

Approaching Temple Meads station a more modern air is portrayed by the colour light signalling – a sign of things to come. Lines swing away to the right leading to the avoiding lines used by freights and summer Saturday trains which pass St. Philip's Marsh shed. The main lines bend to the left and passing under Bath Road bridge the vista of Bath Road shed appears on the right. The young spotter scribbled furiously to record as many numbers as possible in his notebook. All shapes and sizes of GWR passenger types could be seen together with a scattering of standard engines and on occasions even a Britannia.

By the time that the real day's spotting starts there could already be some thirty numbers in the book.

Bristol Temple Meads could be a fascinating place for the spotter with fifteen platforms plus some through roads to keep an eye on. Nearly every train changed engines, those for Birmingham via the Midland route exchanging their Great Western motive power for a Black 5, Jubilee or in the height of the season maybe a Crab or Midland Cl.4F 0-6-0. Alternatively of course the traveller for Birmingham or Wolverhampton could travel via Stratford behind a Stafford Road Castle.

Travellers to Paddington would also usually find a Castle at the head of their train but those to Cardiff or Weymouth would more than likely have a Hall, whilst the North and West route through Pontypool Road and Hereford to Shrewsbury was a frequent haunt of Counties. One GWR class that would cause a stir however would be a Manor, 7808 *Cookham Manor* being the only member to appear with any regularity.

Branch trains also ran to and fro with regularity to Severn Beach, Bath Green Park, Portishead etc. with stopping services on all the main routes as well. The spotters congregated at the Bath Road end of the station catching tantalizing views of the freight traffic passing behind the depot on the avoiding line as well as seeing all the engines being shunted around the depot. 28XX predominated on freight traffic with 73XX, Granges and Halls. The Bristol depots also had a spattering of LMS Cl.8Fs, Austerities and Cl.9Fs to help out, these classes being much more common on the LMR line Northwards to Birmingham and beyond.

The story could go on. But there were the first signs of change, even in 1957. Modernisation had been started by the GWR many years before but had in the main been stopped by the Second World War. However now the schemes were being revived. A few of the GWR railcars worked from Bristol whilst the goods yard adjacent to the North end of the station was being worked by what we would today call Cl.08 class diesel shunters. On the main line regular appearances were made by the Gas Turbine 18000. Few would have believed that in less than ten years steam would have completely gone, for a Sunday visit to the three depots in Bristol would have produced something around 300 steam engines. Of course it was not just the engines at Bristol but the huge concentrations of engines in South Wales, the Midlands,

BRISTOL: Spotters' Paradise. The view from the South end of Bristol Temple Meads of Bath Road Motive Power Depot. Although this picture predates our surveys by two years the Castle taking water, with headcode M96 in place, is on cue (if the shed clock is correct) to take over the 10.05 Penzance-Manchester (train *052*) which would arrive in Bristol at around 16.20, July 9th 1960. *(Hugh Ballantyne)*

London and the South West that would all have gone to the scrap yard, replaced by just a few hundred diesel locomotives and multiple units.

Strange as it may seem, the young spotter seemed to have a preference for spotting in the Summer and so it is that much of this book looks at train services on Summer Saturdays. It seems that those days held a strange fascination for spotters with the seemingly endless procession of trains going to and from distant places and frequently hauled by freight engines or those from unusual depots.

A very interesting book *Summer Saturdays in the West* published by David and Charles, is a useful reference book and starting point for an accurate view of Summer traffic in 1957. This was the final year of 100% steam operation. On 27th July of that year a comprehensive traffic survey of Saturday West Country traffic was undertaken and is described in detail in that book. In order to

present a reasonable comparison with the surveys carried out by the author in later years the David and Charles observations made at Exeter are used as they cover the full period of the day, although the reader will note that Taunton was the focus for the later surveys.

Between 09.00 and 18.00 fifty-six main line trains passed Exeter going South (when comparing this figure with the later years at Taunton the reader should bear in mind that the Taunton movements include the lines to Minehead and Ilfracombe plus some other branch movements).

Starting points for these fifty-six trains were:–

Birmingham Moor Street	2
Birmingham New Street	1
Birmingham Snow Hill	3
Bristol	15
Cardiff	4
Carmarthen	1
Coventry	1
Ealing Broadway	1

BRISTOL: The North end of Bristol Temple Meads. The occupants of the platforms show varying degrees of interest in the unkept St Philip's Marsh Castle 7014 *Caerhayes Castle* as it get to grips with the 11.20 Newquay-Wolverhampton on 17th August 1963. Three weeks previously a Stafford Road engine was in charge (train *199*). Signs of things to come are evident with a Hymek at the adjacent platform.

(Peter W. Gray)

Exeter	2
Kidderminster	1
Leicester	1
Manchester	2
Newport	1
Nottingham	1
Paddington	18
Reading	1
Sheffield	1
Swansea	1
Swindon	1
Taunton	1
Walsall	1
West Bromwich	1
Wolverhampton	5

Motive power comprised:–
Two Counties, twelve Castles, twenty-three Halls, six Granges, one Britannia, four Kings, one Manor; one Pannier Tank (57XX); three 63XX, one 38XX (Parcels), one 41XX and one West Country Pacific.

The West Country was a regular working along the GW route to keep Southern Region crews familiar with the line in case of emergency diversions.

This particular Saturday was seen as one of the most chaotic on record and trains reaching Exeter were around 100 minutes late on average with the 01.28 from Manchester and the 07.25 from Ealing Broadway being around the worst at 165 minutes approximately. A parcels train recorded with 3850 which actually helped cause some of the delays was recorded as being 576 minutes late away from Exeter and 753 minutes late arriving at Plymouth!

Northbound trains in the same period totalled sixty-one. These originated at:–

Churston	1
Exeter	2
Exmouth	1
Falmouth	1
Kingswear	8
Newquay	7
Newton Abbot	2
Paignton	17
Penzance	10
Perranporth	1
Plymouth	5
St. Austell	1
St. Ives	1
Teignmouth	1
Torquay	3

Locomotives used were:–
Counties two, Kings six, 53XX three, Castles nineteen, Halls twenty-one, 47XX one, Granges ten, West Country Pacific one.

Two Northbound trains were double headed. The 47XX was used on a Paddington service.

The lateness of Northbound trains was not so severe and was caused initially by the late arrival of the incoming stock, engine or crew.

Very few of the engines noted passing South through Exeter were seen again during the observation period despite many of them being detached at Newton Abbot. Of the locomotives used further, most had a turnaround time at Newton Abbot of more than four hours.

Castle 5027 *Farleigh Castle* for instance passed Exeter at around 08.30 on the 21.05 Newcastle-Paignton arriving at Newton Abbot at 09.47. It worked forward from Newton Abbot at 14.41 on the 0810 ex-Paddington to Paignton and returned north on the 14.25 Paignton-Sheffield passing Exeter at 16.35 (75 minutes late).

During the period of the 1957 survey engines from distant depots were recorded as Shrewsbury (4), Worcester (4), Hereford (1), Gloucester (1), Stafford Road (2), Oxley (7), Tyseley (2). The Britannia noted (70024) was allocated to Cardiff Canton at this time.

It is suggested in the David and Charles book that 1956 or 1957 marked the zenith of Summer Saturday working in the West and as we shall see it certainly marked the high point of steam activity for the arrival of the diesel hydraulics was just around the corner.

3. Service and Stock Changes

The introduction of the diesel locomotive in the West was decided in the 1955 Modernisation Plan, the idea at that time being to build a number of pilot designs to trial over an extended period. It was envisaged that steam would take some thirty years to phase out and indeed many more steam engines were still on order with a design life of forty years. When looking at 1957 it is worth remembering that the entry into service of the final Cl.9Fs was still three years away – the traveller of 1959 or 1960 could indeed find that the steam engine on the front of the train was built more recently than the diesel on the preceding service.

In the period 1957 to 1960 it became apparent to British Railways that their plans for a proper evaluation of the diesel prototypes was not a feasible scheme, mainly due to the problems of getting staff to work in the dirty inhospitable conditions found in steam engine sheds of the day. Accordingly large orders for completely untried diesel designs were placed.

The Western Region of British Railways had been chosen to evaluate hydraulic transmission in diesel locomotives and orders were placed for three pilot classes of locomotive – two 2,000hp designs for main line work and one of 1,000hp for branch line duties. In addition many diesel multiple units were put under construction which also had their part to play in the demise of steam.

Before the arrival of many of the prototypes further orders were placed, both for similar locomotives and for new classes such that the eventual hydraulic fleet comprised:–

D600-4	Type 4 2,000hp built by North British Locomotive Co. (Warships)
D800-70	Type 4 2,000hp built by British Railways and North British based on a German design (Warships)
D1000-72	Type 4 2,700hp built by British Railways at Swindon and Crewe and derived from the D800 series (Westerns)
D6300-57	Type 2 1,000/1,100hp built by North British Locomotive Co. being almost a mini version of D600-4.
D7000-7100	Type 3 1,750hp built by Beyer Peacock Ltd. (Hymeks)
D9500-55	650hp 'shunting locomotives' built at Swindon.

These locomotives were by no means sufficient to dieselise the whole of the Western Region but around 1962 another decision was taken that diesel electrics were to be the standard for the future. Peak Type 4s were already allocated to Bristol for working London Midland services and subsequently large numbers of English Electric Type 3s and Brush Type 4s were allocated to the Western Region, initially to South Wales. It was a long time, however, before they took over and finally ousted hydraulics from the West Country.

Had the pattern and volume of traffic not changed it is possible that the Western Region would still reverberate with the sound of Maybach engines today but as foreshadowed in the previous chapter times were changing – and rapidly.

The growth of both fast bus services and car ownership combined with the construction of a good road system led to a huge transfer of traffic away from the railways. Up to 1963 this led to the piece-meal withdrawal of a few trains here and there but after the Beeching Report whole lines disappeared and numerous stations closed. The local freight and stopping passenger trains ceased in many parts of the country. British Railways also started to rationalise the main line freight services that it offered and there was a similar drift to road particularly for short freight movements.

No sooner had the last steam engines been ousted from the Western Region therefore when diesels started to become surplus to requirements. As the hydraulics were now non-standard to the rest of the national fleet it meant that, other than the 95XX locomotives, it was the diesel electric locomotives that were moved away and temporarily the hydraulics spread their operations to work all over the system and even took on work on former Southern Region trains to Waterloo. But this was not to last long – even before the final British Railways steam locomotives had been withdrawn the first casualties were seen in the ranks of the diesel hydraulics and it was not long before plans were announced for the total elimination of the breed as traffic continued to shrink and surplus diesel electrics returned to oust the hydraulics and consign them to an early grave.

As a background to the following chapters it is useful to chart the demise of steam in the period 1959-1965 and the subsequent early withdrawal of their successors.

1959 opened with a diesel stock consisting of Warships D600-3 and D800-2. In January 1959 D604 and D6300 were delivered not to mention four Cl.9F 2-10-0s. Other than some accident withdrawals the modern GWR passenger classes remained intact but January saw the withdrawal of two Castles and a Hall went in April. We can mostly assess the impact of dieselisation on freight traffic by watching the withdrawal of eight and ten coupled tender engines as a monitor of what was going on in the lower power types. Throughout 1959 withdrawals of 28XX was geared not to the delivery of diesels but to that of the Cl.9F 2-10-0s. Further diesel deliveries during the year comprised D803-14 and D6301-4/6/7 but the only casualties in the main line steam passenger fleet were a further Castle and Hall.

March 1960 saw the end of 9F deliveries and it is noteworthy that following seven 2-8-0 withdrawals in the first half of 1960 only a further six occurred to the end of June 1962.

By the start of the 1960 Summer timetable Warship deliveries had progressed to D822

SWINDON: The graveyard – not only for steam but in less than ten years' time for many diesels too. Castle 5044 *Earl of Dunraven* and Hall 4957 *Postlip Hall* did not make it to run the summer services of 1962. Swindon 1962.

(Author's Collection)

and Type 2s to D6332, but the passenger fleet still suffered only six casualties (five Castles – including 4073 *Caerphilly Castle* – and one Hall).

Warship deliveries then accelerated with the start of the NBL series with a further sixteen units in stock by the end of 1960 though only two further D63XX were received. It can only be assumed that the troubles experienced with these units kept availability to very low levels, the nett effect on the express steam fleet being two Castles, one Hall and a Grange condemned. Leaving aside the D63XX, forty-five Type 4s were on the books at this time which should have seen about ninety steam withdrawals.

1961 continued in the same vein – at the year end class figures were: D600-4, D800-58/66-70, D1000, D6300-35, D7000-15 but the only steam casualties had been three Castles, eight Halls and two Granges. However we must include in these figures the transfer of the twelve WR Britannias to the Midland Region.

1962 presented an entirely different picture. Warship deliveries were completed in June. D63XX locomotives, which had seen a lull in deliveries recommenced with D6337 in March and the final class member, D6357, arrived in November. Westerns appeared at the rate of one per month from February to June but thereafter deliveries from Crewe joined those from Swindon and four or five locomotives were added to stock in some months. No fewer than fifty-two Hymeks also joined the fleet.

The withdrawal rate of the steam fleet started 1962 at the same leisurely pace as had been seen in 1961 with the demise of two Halls in January and a Castle in February but a taste of what was to come – the withdrawal of the first King – also took place in this month.

From then until the end of the Summer service in the first week of September the pace of withdrawals quickened a little as follows:–

March	one Castle, two Halls
April	five Castles, three Halls, one freight locomotive
May	four Castles, seven Halls, one Grange and one freight engine
June	seven Kings, one Castle, one Hall
July	three Kings, seven Castles, eleven Halls
August	five Castles, five Halls, one freight locomotive plus the transfer of four WD 2-8-0s to the Midland Region.

It should be noted that throughout the period under review the withdrawal of smaller engines used for branch line work and freight trip work and shunting continued apace with the arrival of DMUs and diesel shunters.

The end of the Summer timetable however heralded the largest single withdrawal of WR steam power ever. The September withdrawal list contained thirteen Kings, twenty-six Castles, thirty-five Halls, the first three Counties to be taken out of service and three further WD transfers. October witnessed the passing of only one Castle, three each of Halls and Counties and the first two 47XX 2-8-0s, November two Kings, four Castles, three Halls, one County, three GWR freight locomotives plus six WD 2-8-0s. In December the tally was four Kings, one each of Castle, Hall and freight engines plus two more Counties. In the space of eleven months the Kings had been entirely removed from the scene. It should be noted that activity in the withdrawal of the freight locomotives had accelerated markedly, due mainly to the greater availability of Halls and Granges relieved of their secondary passenger work, but also the impact of the Hymeks on this type of work.

The ins and outs of 1963 were necessarily less dramatic. Western and Hymek deliveries continued although a temporary problem with the Hymeks resulted in only three deliveries from August to November but ten then came on the books in December. Only a handful of each class remained for delivery in 1964. However 1963 was the year in which the diesel electric invasion began with the arrival of English Electric Type 3s mainly for freight work in South Wales. Five units were delivered in March and such was the pace of introduction that eighty-two were at work by the end of the year. Brush Type 4 additions to stock commenced in October with sixteen in stock by the end of December.

At 1st January 1963 the Cambrian and Birmingham divisions of the WR were

SWINDON: Although extinct at the end of 1962, King 6018 *King Henry VI* was reinstated in 1963 to work the class farewell tour from Birmingham to Swindon. It is seen here basking in the spring sunshine in the company of replacement motive power – a pair of Hymeks. 28th April 1963. *(Author's Collection)*

transferred to LMR control. This meant that large numbers of GW engines changed 'owners' and their demise is not recorded in the figures that follow although most of the Counties were gradually transferred back to WR stock.

Withdrawals of Castles and Halls were averaging one to two per month for the former and two to three per month for the latter except for the end of season spurt in September/October and what would appear to be a bookkeeping exercise in December which saw eight Castles, twenty Halls, two Granges and a County struck off the stock. However, it was the freight area which took the brunt of 1963 changes. In the early part of the year transfers out depleted the stock with the departure of two Cl.9Fs to the Southern and thirteen WDs to the Midland, whilst in the

Autumn a further ten Cl.9Fs were transferred away.

No fewer than twenty-six GWR origin 2-8-0 tender engines were condemned but in addition the traditional South Wales freight tanks took a hammering with, for example, twenty-five 42XX, 52XX, 56XX, 66XX and 72XX being condemned in December alone, all these being the victims of the influx of English Electric Type 3s.

The final delivery of Hymeks and Westerns took place in 1964 and Swindon then turned its attention to the production of the D95XX 0-6-0 650h.p. trip and shunting locomotives. These are relevant to the story in as much as some of the work carried out by them had previously been the preserve of D63XX diesels and obviously steam engines so their introduction led to the re-allocation of some

D63XX. Similarly, when they transferred away from the WR only two or three years later the 63XX returned to old haunts to take over their duties. Twenty-four of the 95XX had been put to stock by the end of 1964, together with a further fifty-one English Electric Type 3s (the majority in the early part of the year) and almost one hundred Brush Type 4s, forty-six of which arrived between May and July.

By now the Castles had been severely depleted and a continuing two to three per month coming off service through 1964 ensured only four were in WR stock at the year end. Hall withdrawal rates averaged out at around six per month, although seventeen went for scrap in June. Counties were finally eliminated in November 1964 whilst the Granges based on the Western Region also suffered two to three withdrawals in most months. Somehow the Manors managed to stay intact until 1st May 1964 and the WR stock saw only three depletions in the year.

The real impact was on the freight engines where in a period of about eighteen months virtually all of the South Wales stock was eliminated. The first WR Cl.9F withdrawal took place in February and no fewer than fifty heavy freight tender engines plus numerous large tanks met their end in 1964. Ten Stanier Cl.8F 2-8-0s were more fortunate, these being transferred to the LMR in September.

1965 marked the end of the steam story but it also saw the beginning of the end for the hydraulics as well.

The D95XX class was completed in October 1965 with the arrival of D9555 and the final English Electric Type 3, D6608 was added to stock in November. Cl.47 deliveries slowed, the monthly figures being nine, nine, eight, six and three respectively for the first five months. Deliveries recommenced in September and in fact continued until April 1966, a further forty-four units arriving in this time.

Steam was set to be eliminated at 31st December 1965 from the WR. This in fact did not happen due to a last minute extension to the life of the Somerset and Dorset where a few LMS and Standard engines hung on until March 1966.

7029 *Clun Castle* outlasted its companions by six months to take part in the 'last rites' of steam and was withdrawn in December along with the twenty-three remaining Halls, four Granges, two Manors and seven heavy freight engines. Milestones in 1965 were the withdrawal in March of 92220 *Evening Star* and the first Brush Type 4–D1734 (admittedly this being as a result of an accident).

June saw the withdrawal of fifty-seven pannier tanks. This reflected the huge contraction of the type of work that these engines were designed for as only two D95XX were added to stock in compensation, both DMU and shunter deliveries having ceased by that time.

This contraction could be seen in other indicators – for some time ten Peak Type 4s had been allocated to Bristol to work services to the Midlands and North East. In December 1965 these were moved away, replaced by Brush Type 4s and in addition nine of the Brushes themselves went to the LMR, no doubt all ousting steam elsewhere. In the following months of 1966 this trend continued with a continuous decline in traffic – nine Brush Type 4s transferred out in February, six in April, eleven in May – all to the LMR and English Electric Type 3s – twelve to the NER in May and a start of moves to the Scottish region in July with two examples.

The hydraulics moved to cover for these transfers as it wasn't just in the original diesel electric areas that work was being lost – it was right across the region. It was the continuance of this trend across British Railways in subsequent years that provided spare diesel electrics to start to oust the hydraulics even before the last steam engine had been withdrawn – but that is another story.

The following chapters illustrate the changing scene but a picture can also be seen by looking at reports of visits to works and motive power depots during this time.

An early 1959 visit to Swindon Works produced the following: Under construction were three Cl.9F 2-10-0s, Warships D803-11 and 204hp diesel shunters D2036-41. The only other 'modern' traction present was D604 *Cossack*, six BR 0-6-0 diesel shunters, one of the similar GWR design plus the gas turbine 18000. Steam at works for repair comprised: four Kings, seventeen Castles, four Counties, twenty-two Halls, two Granges, two Britannias and one each of Manors and Standard Cl.5 4-6-0s comprising the passenger classes. Other assorted steam comprised twenty-eight engines. Total steam for repair – eighty-one. No fewer than thirty-six condemned engines were present, mainly tank classes.

One year later little had changed though the building of steam locomotives was about to cease.

The beginning of 1961 had new construction as D831/2/66-70, D1000-6, and D2145/6/87-92. Diesels however were now evident for repair with nine Warships in works, five D63XX, seven shunters and gas turbine 18000. Steam comprised five Kings, eighteen Castles, two each of Manors, Counties and Britannias, eighteen Halls and four Granges. In addition there were forty-five other engines present although a number of these subsequently went for scrap. Therefore the steam total went up, to ninety-six. A similar number of condemned engines were at the works as in 1959.

It was noticeable that one year later D1001 was still under construction in the works in company with D1002-19 and D2183-6. Diesel repairs were down with six Warships only, three D63XX, one Hymek and eight shunters.

Four Kings, fifteen Castles, six Counties, four Granges, one Manor and one Standard Cl.5 comprised the total passenger stock and these were accompanied by forty-four other engines. Some work on Standard classes had been transferred, the Britannias being replaced by Cl.9Fs from other regions, a total of seventy-five 'active' engines plus twenty-two condemned.

A very different sight greeted the 1963 visitor in the depths of an extremely cold and snowy January. Diesel construction comprised D1016-29 and for repair were one Peak Type 4, four Warships, three Westerns, two Hymeks and two shunters. Just five Castles were in works together with nine Halls, six Granges and two Manors. Twenty-eight other engines completed the collection plus eighteen withdrawn. The total of fifty 'active' locomotives showed a 33% reduction in one year and this was on top of the fact that some of the smaller works had closed and their work had moved to Swindon.

The GWR enthusiast of 1964 would find it hard to accept the changes he found on his yearly pilgrimage.

Main line diesel construction was nearly at an end with only D1027-9 being completed although a start had been made on D9500/1. Eight Warships were in for repair and the troubles of the Westerns were evident with eleven representatives at the works. Conversely the success of the Hymeks could be seen with just one locomotive present. The rest of the diesel visitors were one D63XX and six shunters. And what of main line steam? – one Hall, six Granges and one Manor. The other steam engines had a strange look to them comprising Ivatt 2-6-0s, Standard Cl.3s, and Stanier 2-6-0s, making a total of only thirty-six 'active' steam with around twenty withdrawn.

A similar visit in 1965 found just fifteen steam engines between the works and shed and some of these were for preservation.

The pattern was repeated with depot visits in Bristol.

16th March 1963
Barrow Road – forty-nine steam (fourteen of GWR origin)
St. Philips Marsh – forty-eight steam of which twenty-six were of the passenger classes (but only two Castles).

21st March 1964
Barrow Road – fifty-one steam (twenty-one of GWR origin)
St. Philips Marsh – thirty-seven steam – twenty-five passenger types but no fewer than eight Castles showing the relegation of these engines to lesser duties.

17th January 1965
Barrow Road – fifty-eight steam (twenty-four of GWR origin)
St. Philips Marsh – Closed. The GW engines now stabled at Barrow Road and nine passenger engines were present.

23rd October 1965
Barrow Road – twenty-five steam (eight of GWR origin) of which five were passenger engines.

On the same date Bath Road was visited – the modern day enthusiast may be surprised to learn that only ten diesel hydraulics were on shed.

Until the closure of St. Philips Marsh the GWR types using Barrow Road were all shunting engines with the occasional 63XX or 28XX. The decline of LMR steam power can also be seen from these observations, being thirty-five in 1963 including three Jubilees, thirty in 1964 (one Jubilee) and seventeen in 1965 when Stanier Black 5s were the largest passenger type on show.

The WR dieselisation programme was completed first in the South West followed by the Bristol area (excluding Gloucester), then West Wales. This was then extended to the rest of the WR area in Wales, together with the area to the north of Bristol and the remaining local steam in the London motive power area. A visit to Taunton in July 1963 produced a diesel/steam ratio of 5:1 whilst a few weeks later in South Wales equal steam and diesel numbers were noted and this included the counting of individual DMU cars!

The mixed state of dieselisation in the London area was illustrated by an Old Oak Common visit in April of 1964. Two Warships were visiting the depot, along with eleven Westerns, nine Brush Type 4s, eight Hymeks and two D63XX (total thirty-two). Fifty-four steam engines shared the accommodation of which twenty-two were main line types.

In March 1965, with only nine months left for the region's steam, Southall was still host to more than sixty steam locomotives although most of these were tank or freight classes (Old Oak was diesel only by this time).

The picture had been repeated around the region – passenger steam replaced by diesels combined with line closures saw steam numbers reduced. At the same time some of the surviving passenger types moved over to freight work but were still available to be called on as diesel stand-ins as required. The arrival of the diesel electrics heralded the end of the steam freight. As freight traffic continued to decline the hydraulics were spread further around the region to release diesel electrics for use in other regions to continue the dieselisation process.

4. Taunton Traffic 1962-1965

In this and the following three chapters, we shall see how the locomotive scene changed on a specific Saturday in successive years, with the aid of traffic surveys. The observers were at Taunton, Bristol, Gloucester and on the South Wales line. Each train has been allocated a unique number which can be followed through the various observation points and these are referred to here, rather than train reporting numbers. The traffic surveys for each location may be found at the end of the relevant chapter.

Looking firstly at Taunton we can follow motive power on the Paddington - Westbury - South West route and working south from Bristol. The survey dates were 28th July 1962, 27th July 1963, 25th July 1964 and 21st August 1965 (ie four weeks later). Fortunately the first three years tie in very well with the 1957 survey referred to earlier. The unique reference numbers are shown in italics in the text.

TAUNTON: In 1962 steam type headboards were still in use on Western Region named trains. Indeed, on some occasions of diesel shortage various named trains would still be steam worked. D822 *Hercules* is seen approaching Cogload Junction to the north of Taunton on 2nd June 1962. The lines from Bristol and Paddington, via Westbury, come together at Cogload. *(R. E. Toop)*

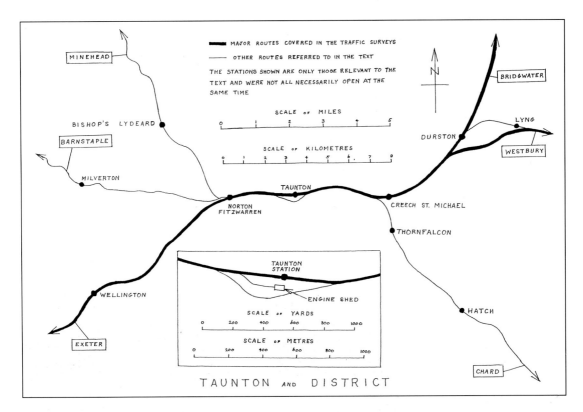

TAUNTON AND DISTRICT

4.1. Paddington – South West

1962 Survey

Observation time 09.30-19.20

Southbound

The destinations of trains originating at Paddington were: Penzance seven, Kingswear four, Paignton four (one via Bristol), Minehead three, and one each for Truro, Perranporth, Falmouth and Plymouth, Total twenty-two. Motive power: Penzance services five Warships, one Western, one King (6021 *King Richard II*); Paignton three Warships, one Hall (6953 *Leighton Hall*); Plymouth – Castle 7021 *Haverfordwest Castle*; all other services except Minehead: Warship. No D6XX series were recorded on any of the survey dates.

Minehead services. Train *090* arriving at Taunton at 10.45 was worked in by Grange 6856 *Stowe Grange* of Worcester which gave way to 41XX 4128 at Taunton. The second train was headed by an old Oak Castle, 4143 working forward, whilst the third train (arrival 13.11) produced King 6026 *King John*. 61XX 6155 took over for the branch journey.

Many of the services loaded to fourteen coaches whilst the "Cornish Riviera Express" *(train 109)* had fifteen on with Western power.

Trains to Paddington

No fewer than twenty-five trains were recorded.

Starting points were: Paignton four, Newquay two; Plymouth two, Kingswear three; Falmouth, Churston, Torquay, Newton Abbot, Truro and Taunton one each; with five originating at Penzance. In addition there were three services from Minehead (however the first was amalgamated with a train from Plymouth and so is not counted separately).

Motive power was similar to the down services with D8XX series Warships working all except the following:

D1000 *Western Enterprise* came up on train *012* from Truro at 10.45 whilst Hymek D7016 (Bath Road) worked train *064* which originated at Taunton at 16.50. The Minehead trains were worked by 41XX or 61XX. The first train went forward behind a Warship hauled service from Plymouth and the third

TAUNTON: By 1963 Warships with yellow warning panels and rakes of maroon stock were very much the regular scene South of Bristol. Devoid of any identification other than the reporting number the *Cornish Riviera Express* approaches Taunton from the South passing the goods yards and carriage sidings. The locomotive on 27th April 1963 was D818 *Glory*. (*R. E. Toop*)

was a return working for 6026. The locomotive for the second train was not identified.

A locomotive failure occurred on train *026* from Paignton when D812 *Royal Naval Reserve 1859-1959* had to be replaced at Taunton by Hall 6907 *Davenham Hall* allocated to Oxley. This was probably due to work the later Minehead and Ilfracombe-Wolverhampton.

1963 Survey
Paddington line (Observation times as for 1962)
Down trains
Eighteen were recorded, a drop of four over 1962.
Destinations were:- Penzance, four; Minehead, three; Plymouth, two; Kingswear, two; Truro, Dartmouth, Falmouth and Newquay, one each; Paignton, four.

Only one Western appeared, again on a Penzance service (but not the Cornish Riviera Express) but five Hymeks were utilized being

allocated to Old Oak Common (four) and Bath Road (one). They appeared, one on a Kingswear train and on Paignton and Minehead services, two each. The onward services to Minehead were in the hands of a D63XX, 41XX 2-6-2 tank and a Bath Road Hymek. Loads were generally about one coach less than 1962.

Up trains
Twenty-three were recorded (two down on 1962). Minehead line – as in the previous year three trains originated there, with the first on this occasion being combined with a Paignton service. Four trains started there, five at Penzance, two each at Dartmouth, Kingswear and Newquay and one each from Truro, Churston, Plymouth, Falmouth, Newton Abbot and Taunton.

The solitary Western worked up from Falmouth whilst Hymeks were in charge of one Kingswear service, one Paignton and the

19

Newton Abbot and Taunton services. All were Bath Road locomotives except the Kingswear which was a return Old Oak working.

The inward Minehead services reflected the outward workings other than the 41XX tank was double-headed with a 57XX pannier tank. Warships were responsible for all other services.

1964 Survey

The observation period was reduced to an 18.15 finish. As far as Paddington services are concerned this would eliminate two Northbound workings and the Down Truro service.

Seventeen Down services were recorded with a marked change in motive power on show.

Destinations: Kingswear three, Penzance four, Paignton four, Minehead two, Newquay one, Plymouth one and two unknown but probably not the Torbay branch.

Unlike the previous years Warships were in the minority with only four being used on these services. Hymeks were to be found on one Kingswear working (Bath Road allocated), Paignton three (two from Old Oak and one from Canton) and both Minehead services (Old Oak engines). Westerns by this time were allocated to a range of depots and Landore, Canton and Bath Road machines were to be seen as well as Plymouth locomotives. The Landore example was one of three Westerns working to Penzance, with the balance of the Kingswear services, one Paignton and both the 'unknown' trains being handled by this class as well. One Minehead train went forward behind a D63XX whilst the second set a new working pattern with the Hymek that brought it into Taunton, working through.

Only nineteen Northbound trains were noted comprising five from Paignton (one taking forward a Minehead portion), four from Penzance, three from Kingswear, two from Newquay and one each from Plymouth, Falmouth and Newton Abbot, along with two through Minehead trains. Hymeks were to be found on the Minehead trains onwards from Taunton (one through engine working) and two on Paignton workings (both Bath Road engines). Westerns were to be found on one Paignton train (Landore allocated), one Kingswear, the Plymouth, Falmouth, both Newquays and three of the four from Penzance. Other trains were worked by

Warships, the Newton Abbot train having changed over from the 1963 Hymek.

1965 Survey

For the final year of these surveys it must be noted that the survey date was one month later, the duration of the survey being the same as 1964.

Only one Minehead through service ran in the Down direction, but a new destination was Ilfracombe which had three services. These ran via Exeter replacing services provided from Waterloo in previous years. Penzance had six trains, Paignton and Kingswear two each and one each to Falmouth, Newquay, Dartmouth and Plymouth – total eighteen. Many trains had loadings of fourteen coaches again. The solitary Minehead train exchanged Hymeks, the locomotive working forward being one of the small batch allocated to Laira. Ilfracombe trains had the services of one each of Warship, Western and Hymek, the Dartmouth also utilising an Old Oak Hymek. The only recorded Penzance working with a Hymek had a Bath Road example, the sole Plymouth train also being Hymek worked by Old Oak Common.

Westerns were in charge of four trains to Penzance, one of the Paigntons, as well as the Falmouth and Newquay turns with D800 series Warships on the rest.

Finally the Up Paddington services can be presented. The combined Minehead and Paignton service saw Hymeks on both parts. There was only one other Minehead service, with a Laira Hymek working through. There were three balancing trains originating from Ilfracombe – two with Hymeks and one Western. Other origins were Kingswear (two), Penzance (five), Paignton (four in addition to the combined train), Newquay (two), Dartmouth and Newton Abbot one each.

Hymeks were to be found on one Kingswear train, one Paignton and the Newton Abbot service with Westerns on three from Penzance, both Newquays and one Paignton service. All other workings on the route were Warship hauled.

As far as the Paddington line is concerned therefore we can see that the initial ousting of steam took place between mid-1960, when a visit to Taunton at the end of June produced a total of seven Warships, and the start of the

TAUNTON: All the Western Region attempts at individualism (except the locomotive design) had been eradicated by the end of the 1960s. The maroon livery of the Westerns had been changed to Standard Blue (those surviving in maroon at this time looked distinctly rough) and the chocolate and cream carriages had long been replaced, first by maroon, and then by rail blue and grey. The Warships had also started to go for scrap along with the North British 63XX types whilst the Westerns were half way through their reign. D1038 *Western Sovereign* in blue livery heads the 10.46 Newton Abbot-Paddington at Fairwood Junction near Westbury. 12th July 1969. *(Hugh Ballantyne)*

1962 Summer timetable.

Despite the fact that around fifty each of Westerns and Hymeks had been delivered before the 1963 survey, it was not until 1964 that their real impact was seen on this route. Steam did not feature on Paddington services after 1962 other than as a stand-in for a diesel failure.

4.2. Bristol Line Traffic

Turning our attention to this route to the South West it is convenient to split the traffic into three sub-groups, viz that using the Severn Tunnel, trains via Gloucester and 'the rest', being very few, going to Bristol and local destinations. This will allow for comparison with the surveys taken on these lines, detailed in later chapters. Motive power used beyond Bristol will be analysed there.

1962 Survey
Southbound via the Severn Tunnel

Two trains reached Taunton that passed the South Wales survey point before the surveyor arrived, although they were noted at Bristol. Train *082* with Hall 6981 *Marbury Hall* and train *086* with Bath Road Hymek D7012 originated respectively at Cardiff and Newport. These were followed by train *094* (Cardiff-Kingswear). At 11.19 an unidentified train for Kingswear passed with Hall 6903 *Belmont Hall* of

21

Pontypool Road in charge, then Warship worked train *111*, Carmarthen-Penzance. Next came a Swansea-Minehead and Swansea-Kingswear, the former with a Hall from Bristol handing over to a 41XX at Taunton. The latter, routed via St. Philips Marsh to avoid Temple Meads, was Hymek worked.

A Treherbert-Paignton was noted with a Laira Castle which worked right through, presumably from Cardiff, then train *118* (Carmarthen-Penzance) with a Warship, Cardiff-Newquay (Warship), Manchester-Penzance (Warship throughout from Shrewsbury), Liverpool-Paignton (Hymek), Manchester-Paignton and Liverpool-Plymouth (both Warships) and finally the Manchester-Plymouth being another through turn for a Warship.

Northbound via the Severn Tunnel
The day started with a Newton Abbot-Swansea working, this being the only main line DMU turn on this route. Following were a Paignton-Cardiff (Hymek), Exeter-Manchester (Warship), Paignton-Manchester (Warship through to Shrewsbury), and Minehead and Ilfracombe-Manchester worked by a Hall from Taunton. The Minehead portion came in behind a 57XX tank and that from Ilfracombe behind 2-6-0 6327. Following were Penzance-Liverpool (through Warship turn) and Paignton-Carmarthen (Hymek). Next came a Minehead and Barnstaple to Cardiff, the former brought in by 4174 and the latter by 7337. This train was unusually worked forward by D812 *Royal Naval Reserve 1859-1959* which had failed earlier on an up Paddington service. Two Manchester trains followed with a Warship from Newquay and a Hymek from Kingswear.

Train *040*, Paignton-Cardiff, produced a Newton Abbot Castle with a Hymek on train *046* Kingswear-Manchester. A further Warship turn was the through working on train *052* (Penzance-Manchester) which was followed by train *061* (Penzance-Swansea) with a Warship, Newquay-Cardiff (Warship) and Kingswear-Cardiff (Hymek). The final working was the Penzance-Glasgow again with a Warship.

Southbound from Gloucester
The first train observed (only at Taunton) was *099* Wolverhampton-Paignton with a Bath Road Hymek probably running via St Philips Marsh. Next came a twelve coach Walsall-Kingswear (Hymek) and a Wolverhampton-Penzance with a Warship. Train *106* (Leicester-Paignton) followed.

All these trains were observed at Bristol and Taunton only, the Gloucester observer not arriving until 11.15. Nottingham-Plymouth (Warship), Sheffield-Paignton and Wolverhampton-Kingswear (both Hymek worked) were next. Then followed an unidentified service *(123)* worked by Hall 6965 *Thirlestaine Hall*. A further Hymek turn was the Wolverhampton-Minehead and Ilfracombe with a 41XX working forward to Minehead and a 73XX to Ilfracombe.

Train *134* (Newcastle-Paignton) was hauled by a Warship, the following Bradford-Paignton by a Hymek *(135)* and a second similar train *(142)* by a Warship.

Northbound via Gloucester
The first train *(002)* was Paignton-Newcastle with a Warship, followed by a Paignton-Derby having the services of Hall 6987 *Shervington Hall* whilst the Paignton-Nottingham *(007)* and Paignton-Leeds *(010)* were in the hands of Hymeks. The Devonian (Kingswear-Bradford) was hauled by a Warship but both the Newton Abbot-Bradford and Kingswear-Wolverhampton again had Hymeks. Train *030*, Newquay-Newcastle, had a Warship and the following Paignton-Nottingham yet another Hymek.

The Minehead and Ilfracombe to Wolverhampton was provided with a 41XX from the former and 73XX from Ilfracombe. These gave way to Penzance County 1006 *County of Cornwall* which worked through and must have raised a few eyebrows north of Bristol. (This is the train that 6907 was probably due to work before having to stand in for D812 on the Paddington working *(026)*).

The diet of Warships was resumed with Penzance-Bradford *(043)* and Hymeks with the Paignton-Wolverhampton. The Newquay-Wolverhampton passed Taunton in the charge of Hall 6905 *Claughton Hall* and somewhere en route to Bristol D827 *Kelly* was collected. Newquay-York was Warship hauled as was the following Penzance-Wolverhampton but the Paignton-Wolverhampton (train *058*) was a

Hymek. Train *062* (Paignton-Sheffield) was also a Hymek with a Warship on the final Wolverhampton service *(067)*.

Other Taunton Services

Southbound a regular opening train was the Bristol-Penzance with a Warship and this was the only main line passenger working not dealt with above with the exception of unidentified service *097*. Two parcels trains were recorded, one with 2-8-0 3810, the second having a Warship. Other services involved the local stopping trains and branch line traffic.

These included Taunton-Minehead and Ilfracombe trips with similar motive power to the main line services. Also to be seen were Yeovil and Castle Cary services plus Taunton-Exeter. The Exeter trains had main line steam power except for one DMU with the locals utilising 41XX, 57XX, 55XX and Standard tank 82044.

Northbound a similar pattern was seen but the day was rounded off by a steam hauled ECS with County 1009 *County of Carmarthen.*

Although a survey was not carried out at Taunton in 1961 a part survey was conducted at Worle Junction North of Weston-super-Mare on the corresponding date, 29th July. Trains were observed for two hours in both the morning and afternoon and four Warships only were recorded, these working the Northbound Devonian and the 10.05 Penzance-Manchester whilst southbound the 12.21 Cardiff-Newquay was followed down by 08.00 Manchester-Penzance. Virtually all other services noted were worked by either Halls or Granges.

1963 Survey
Severn Tunnel route
The 1962 steam hauled service from Newport to Paignton did not run in 1963 but the following train, 227, was again Hymek worked. The Cardiff-Kingswear service materialised as train *231* being a fifteen coach DMU – twelve of these working to Kingswear but the other three were detached at Bristol to work only as far as Weston-super-Mare. The Swansea to Minehead of 1962 also had an Ilfracombe portion in 1963 with Hymek haulage from Bristol but was still steam worked forward

from Taunton (41XX to Minehead, 53XX to Ilfracombe).

Other changes from 1962 were that the Treherbert train did not run, and the Penzance train originated at Carmarthen. The Cardiff-Newquay only ran to Newton Abbot and the Liverpool-Kingswear (train *266*) had previously terminated at Paignton, all other motive power was as in 1962.

Northbound the DMU turn was diverted to Porthcawl instead of Swansea. The Paignton-Cardiff working did not run and the Exeter-Manchester started back at Exmouth with a Hymek.

The Minehead and Ilfracombe train retained its steam haulage even to the extent that 6327 was again on the Ilfracombe portion. Following a Paignton-Carmarthen there was an additional service to Preston (train *173*) with a Bath Road Hymek.

Due to an engine failure the Minehead portion, to be combined with that from Ilfracombe going forward to Cardiff, was hauled by a Standard Cl.3 tank. A Hall worked on from Taunton. In place of a Castle on the Paignton-Cardiff, D7021 performed. Train *193* originated at Paignton (previously Kingswear). Only three of the previous year's five final trains appeared, viz Penzance-Swansea (Warship), Kingswear-Cardiff (DMU) and Penzance-Glasgow. Motive power was as in 1962 unless stated otherwise.

Gloucester Line
Southbound one train, identified as Sheffield-Penzance, entry *258*, evaded recorders further North (probably running via St Philips Marsh) to arrive at Taunton at 14.11 being Warship hauled.

The first train recorded at Bristol was a relief Walsall-Kingswear (*233*) with a Hymek followed by the main train (*236*), thence Leicester-Paignton (*249*) and Wolverhampton-Minehead and Ilfracombe. On this occasion the train engine worked through to Minehead with a 53XX on the Ilfracombe portion.

The Gloucester observer again started at 11.15 and recorded the Nottingham-Plymouth, which being of only seven coaches was downgraded to Hymek haulage South of Bristol. IV36 did not run, the only other variance recorded being that one of the

Bradford trains preceded the Newcastle. Other trains and motive power were as 1962.

Variances on the first four Northbound trains were a Hymek on the Paignton-Derby (train *156*) with the Leeds service being cut back to Sheffield.

The Minehead and Ilfracombe service again produced a 53XX from Ilfracombe but a D63XX from Minehead with a Banbury based Hall forward from Taunton. An additional Paignton-Sheffield service with Hymek haulage followed the Penzance-Bradford. Newquay-Wolverhampton did not produce steam in 1963, being worked by a Warship. Train *202*, Penzance-Sheffield, with class leader D800 *Sir Brian Robertson* came Up next. The final Paignton-Birmingham was downgraded to Hymek haulage. Other workings were unchanged.

Taunton Local Workings

The Bristol-Penzance service was handled again by a Warship but other local services were extremely sparse. The one Taunton-Exeter was Hymek worked, a Taunton-Newton Abbot was a DMU as were Taunton-Minehead locals. The only steam engine noted working through to Exeter was 4707 on parcels at 18.30 (*281*).

1964 Survey

Remarkably – in view of the changes seen during 1962 and 1963 – steam hung on at Taunton for a further year.

Southbound via the Severn Tunnel

Cardiff-Paignton (Hymek) and Cardiff-Kingswear (only a nine car DMU on this occasion) opened the recording. The Minehead-Ilfracombe service was Hymek worked to Taunton, one Hymek being exchanged for another on the Minehead portion. Strange motive power took over the Ilfracombe portion – Cl.N 31406 of Exmouth Junction.

The following three services all produced Hymeks the latter being a Carmarthen-Taunton turn. Although most of the trains from the North and West route produced Warships the practice of these working through from Shrewsbury had ceased. *389* Liverpool-Kingswear produced the first

Western on a cross country service.

Northbound via the Severn Tunnel

The Newton Abbot-Swansea DMU again opened the account with the Hymek hauled Paignton-Manchester (*288*) following. A new variation was the combining of an Ilfracombe portion with the Exmouth-Manchester train at Taunton with Hymek power on the through service and a D63XX on the branch train.

Warships featured on the following trains to the North-West but as in the case of Southbound workings they were replaced at Bristol.

The Ilfracombe and Minehead-Cardiff service had a Hymek working through from Minehead but had a 53XX allocated to Severn Tunnel Junction on the Ilfracombe portion.

The Hymek/Warship pattern was evident on most other services. An exception was an extra to Preston (*325*) which came North with D1003 *Western Pioneer* and the final Kingswear-Cardiff which was DMU worked.

Southbound via Gloucester

Wolverhampton-Dartmouth and Walsall-Kingswear services (both ran in duplicate) followed by a Wolverhampton-Penzance, Leicester-Paignton and Wolverhampton-Minehead/Ilfracombe all passed Gloucester before the observer arrived and all featured Hymek haulage South of Bristol, the train locomotive working through to Minehead on the latter. The Ilfracombe portion ex-Wolverhampton was worked forward by a 53XX from Taunton.

The next two trains (Sheffield-Penzance and Nottingham-Plymouth) featured Warships but the following three services were Hymek worked thence Warship, Hymek and finally a further Warship.

Northbound via Gloucester

The first service (Paignton-Newcastle) was headed by a Warship whilst Paignton-Nottingham was Hymek worked. An unusual sight on an eleven coach Paignton-Leeds was a pair of Hymeks. The Northbound Devonian produced the usual Warship but Western power was provided for Kingswear-Wolverhampton. D63XX power was provided for the Minehead portion and 53XX on the Ilfracombe section of the through train to

Wolverhampton which went forward from Taunton with a Hymek.

Warships were then the order of the day until train *337* Paignton-Wolverhampton with a Hymek, the other two West Midlands trains being Warship and Hymek hauled respectively.

Other Taunton Services

The Minehead branch was totally diesel worked, mainly by Hymeks with the occasional DMU. Most Barnstaple and Ilfracombe services were steam and these were the only steam turns noted. The parcels which produced the only steam turn South of Taunton in 1963 was in the hands of a Warship. Taunton-Exeter locals had ceased and only the DMU worked Taunton-Bristol locals remained.

1965 Survey (NB: Survey date 4 weeks later)
Southbound via the Severn Tunnel

The opening services from Cardiff were both Hymek worked, the DMU through working having ceased. Llanelli-Penzance was a Warship, with Carmarthen-Paignton and Cardiff-Ilfracombe/ Minehead both being Hymeks. The Minehead portion exchanged Hymeks at Taunton and a D63XX was provided for Ilfracombe.

Warships were employed on the next two trains from the North and West route with a Hymek on the Carmarthen-Taunton, a Western on Manchester-Penzance (train *507*) and a further Warship on train *508*. Another first was recorded with a Hymek being added as a pilot from Taunton. Warships were also used for the final two southbound workings.

Northbound via the Severn Tunnel

The DMU working of former years (IF18) had super power in 1965 with a Western with eight coaches. D6331 brought in the Ilfracombe portion to be attached to the Exmouth-Manchester which was Hymek worked. The Penzance-Manchester *(421)* had a Western as did *430* (Kingswear-Manchester), D6333 (Ilfracombe) and D7002 (Minehead) were used for the combined through service to Cardiff which D7002 took forward. A third Western worked *441* (Penzance-Manchester), Warship and Hymeks covering the other turns except for the Western worked Penzance-Liverpool *(468)*.

Southbound via Gloucester

Hymeks again dominated the first Southbound workings although possibly because the survey was carried out four weeks later no reliefs were seen. For the first time both Minehead and Ilfracombe portions of the service from Wolverhampton went forward with D63XX from Taunton. A Western was used for the first time on a service from this route with D1044 *Western Duchess* on Nottingham-Paignton *(497)* and they must have had good availability on this date as extra train *502* also was headed by one, though, Warships and Hymeks were used on the other services as usual.

Northbound via Gloucester

A reduced programme operated and it was not until train *435* appeared at Taunton at 13.20 (Newquay-Manchester) that the Warship/ Hymek pattern was broken with D1009 *Western Invader* in charge. The following Minehead/ Ilfracombe-Wolverhampton was noted with D6348 from Ilfracombe, D7020 from Minehead and D7087 forward from Taunton. Warships predominated on the other afternoon workings.

Other Taunton Workings

Steam was no longer to be seen. DMU workings seemed to have increased with turns on Ilfracombe services and more D63XX were in evidence.

As a summary it can be said that the 1965 services showed the largest changes with several trains being withdrawn. One apparent casualty was IM96 Plymouth-Manchester – this was unfortunate as in 1962, 1963 and 1964 it appeared behind D823 *Hermes* at 15.23, 15.13 and 15.38 respectively. In 1965 IM96 became a Penzance to Manchester worked by D1072 *Western Glory* arriving at 14.06.

Of the survey locations Taunton became the first to lose both main line steam and then to be completely devoid of steam. The casual observer might conclude that Hymeks were the mainstay of West of England services – yet on Monday-Friday passenger services they rarely appeared South of Taunton. The gradual replacement of Warships by Westerns was already under way. It would not be long before diesel electrics would become dominant at this location.

TABLE ONE

SURVEY POINT: TAUNTON – NORTHBOUND – DATE 28th JULY 1962

P = Passing time

Train Ref. No.	Rep. No.	Time	Description	Motive power	Name	Allocation	Arr.	Dep.	Remarks
001	2C70	07.45	Newton Abbot-Swansea	DMU		—	09.27	09.34	
002	IN61	07.45	Paignton-Newcastle-u-Tyne	D831	Monarch	83A	09.44	09.47	
003	IA27	07.45	Kingswear-Paddington	D830	Majestic	83A	10p15		
004	—		Minehead-Paddington	6155		83B	10.01		Added to train 006
005	IM05		Paignton-Derby	6987	Shervington Hall	84A	10.07	10.10	45659 (55A) worked from Bristol. Not recorded at Gloucester
006	IA33	07.30	Plymouth Paddington	D848	Sultan	83A	10.12	10.28	Minehead portion added (004)
007	IM08	08.20	Paignton-Nottingham	D7041		82A	10.16	10.19	
008	IT25	08.33	Paignton-Cardiff	D7008		82A	10.27	10.31	
009	IA36	08.45	Paignton-Paddington	D843	Sharpshooter	83A	10p33		
010	IE67	09.00	Paignton-Leeds	D7020		82A	10p38		
011	IM90	10.00	Exeter-Manchester	D814	Dragon	83D	10p41		
012	IA41	06.45	Truro-Paddington	D1000	Western Enterprise	83D	10.45	10.51	
013	IM89	09.12	Paignton-Manchester	D849	Superb	83A	11p00		
014	IM14		Minehead-Manchester	9670		83B	11.01		Added to train 015
015	IM14	08.35	Ilfracombe-Manchester	6327		83B	11.08		Minehead portion added (014)
				5958	Knolton Hall	82B		11.20	5958 replaced 6327 at Taunton
016	IM91	06.10	Penzance-Liverpool	D825	Intrepid	83A	11p16		
017	IA43	09.45	Churston-Paddington	D845	Sprightly	83A	11p28		
018	IN37	09.00	Kingswear-Bradford	D806	Cambrian	83D	11p36		
019			Barnstaple-Taunton	6372		83B	11.39		
020	IA45	09.30	Plymouth-Paddington	D870	Zulu	83D	12p11		
021	IN40	10.19	Newton Abbot-Bradford	D7005		82A	12.22	12.26	
022		11.15	Minehead-Paddington	4103		83B	12.25	12.40	Engine forward from Taunton not known
023	IA49	10.40	Torquay-Paddington	D841	Roebuck	83A	12p29		
024	IH22	10.05	Kingswear-Wolverhampton	D7016		82A	12p34		
025	IF30	10.15	Paignton-Carmarthen	D7001		82A	12p44		
026	IA51	11.10	Paignton-Paddington	D812	The Royal Naval Reserve 1859-1959	83D	12.55		6907 replaced D812 due to locomotive failure
				6907	Davenham Hall	84B		13.14	

TABLE ONE (continued)

Train Ref. No.	Rep. No.	Time		Description	Motive power	Name	Allocation	Time Arr.	Dep.	Remarks
027	—	08.00		Barnstaple-Cardiff	7337		83B	12.57		Added to train 033
028	1M95	10.45		Newquay-Manchester	D828	*Magnificent*	83A		12p59	
029	1M93	08.43		Kingswear-Manchester	D7017		82A		13p05	
030	1N86	07.30		Newquay-Newcastle	D850	*Swift*	83D		13p13	
031	1A65	11.35		Penzance-Paddington	D864	*Zambesi*	83D		13p22	
032	1N26	12.05		Paignton-Nottingham	D7006		82A	13.29	13.33	
033	—			Minehead-Cardiff	4174		82D	13.32		Barnstaple portion added (027)
					D812	*The Royal Naval Reserve 1859-1959*			13.59	D812 replaced 4174 at Taunton
034	1A66	11.20		Kingswear-Paddington	D865	*Zealous*	83D		13p40	
035	—			Ilfracombe-Wolverhampton	7333		83D	13.44		Added to train 038
036	1A67	09.20		Falmouth-Paddington	D832	*Onslaught*	83B		13p57	
037	—			Exeter-Taunton	DMU		83A	13.58		
038	—	12.45		Minehead-Wolverhampton	4128		83B	14.02		Ilfracombe portion added (035)
					1006	*County of Cornwall*	83G		14.15	1006 replaced 4128 at Taunton
039	1A72	12.32		Newton Abbot-Paddington	D811	*Daring*	83D	14.04	14.08	
040	1T35			Paignton-Cardiff	5055	*Earl of Eldon*	83A	14.14	14.21	Not recorded at Patchway
041				Taunton-Yeovil	8745		72C	14.18	14.23	Arrival as E.C.S.
042	1A75	10.00		Newquay-Paddington	D816	*Eclipse*	83D		14p23	
043	1N68	09.05		Penzance-Bradford	D810	*Cockade*	83D	14.28	14.33	
044	—			Minehead-Taunton	4143		83B	14.29		
045	1A81	09.45		Penzance-Paddington	D853	*Thruster*	83D		14p32	
046	1M97	12.00		Kingswear-Manchester	D7021		82A	14.40	14.45	
047	—			Taunton-Bristol	DMU				14.42	
048	1A83	13.28		Paignton-Paddington	D808	*Centaur*	83D		14p55	
049	—			Barnstaple-Taunton	7304		83B	14.56		
050	1H31	12.55		Paignton-Wolverhampton	D7012		82A	15.03	15.05	
051	1A86	10.40		Penzance-Paddington	D836	*Powerful*	83A		15p13	
052	1M96	10.05		Penzance-Manchester	D823	*Hermes*	83D	15.20	15.23	
053	1H34	11.20		Newquay-Wolverhampton	6905	*Claughton Hall*	86G		15p23	D827 attached en route to Bristol
054	1A89	14.20		Minehead-Paddington	4110		83B	15.24		6026 replaced 4110 at Taunton
					6026		81A		15.37	
055	—			Taunton-Yeovil	5563	*King John*	83B	15.50	16.15	Arrival E.C.S.

TABLE ONE (continued)

Train Ref. No.	Rep. No.	Time	Description	Motive power	Name	Allocation	Time Arr.	Time Dep.	Remarks
056	IN87	11.35	Newquay-York	D867	*Zenith*	83D		15p52	
057	IA92	13.30	Kingswear-Paddington	D803	*Albion*	83D		15p59	
058	IH33	14.15	Paignton-Wolverhampton	D7027		82A		16p12	
059	—		Minehead-Taunton	6155		83B	16.13		
060	IH37	10.50	Penzance-Wolverhampton	D858	*Valorous*	83D		16p20	
061	IF59	11.10	Penzance-Swansea	D817	*Foxhound*	83D		16p22	
062	IE70	14.40	Paignton-Sheffield	D7009		82A	16.37	16.45	
063	M	12.30	Newquay-Paddington	D807	*Caradoc*	83D		16p43	
064	IA33	16.42	Taunton-Paddington	D7016		82A		16.50	via Bristol
065	IA11	15.00	Paignton-Paddington	D856	*Trojan*	83D		16p53	
066	IA12	11.50	Penzance-Paddington	D804	*Avenger*	83D	17.09	17.11	
067	IH44	15.20	Paignton-Wolverhampton	D826	*Jupiter*	83A	17p15		Worked forward from Bristol by 6929 (84C)
068	IT41	12.42	Newquay-Cardiff	D802	*Formidable*	83D	17.21	17.25	
069	—		Minehead-Taunton	4103		83B	17.27		
070	—		Milk train	6372		83B	17.41	18.20	
071	—		Barnstaple-Taunton	6327		83B	17.41		
072	IT45	15.20	Kingswear-Cardiff	D7027		82A	17.48	17.53	
073	IM99	12.00	Penzance-Glasgow	D869	*Zest*	83D	17.59	18.09	
074	—		Minehead-Taunton	4174		82D	18.15		
075	IA32	16.10	Kingswear-Paddington	D829	*Magpie*	83A	18.18	18.24	
076	IA38	13.50	Penzance-Paddington	D863	*Warrior*	83D	18.39	18.44	
077	—		Taunton-Bristol	DMU				18.42	
078	—		Minehead-Taunton	4128		83B	19.06		
079	IC66		E.C.S.	1009	*County of Carmarthen*	82B	19.09	19.20	

TABLE TWO

SURVEY POINT: TAUNTON – SOUTHBOUND – DATE 28th JULY 1962

P = Passing time

Train Ref. No.	Rep. No.	Time	Description	Motive power	Name	Allocation	Arr.	Dep.	Remarks
080	IC22	06.30	Paddington-Penzance	D862	Viking	83D	09.30	09.36	
081	IC58	07.00	Paddington-Kingswear	D811	Daring	83D		09p38	
082	IC55	06.35	Cardiff-Paignton	6981	Marbury Hall	82B	09.40	09.45	
083	IC66	06.55	-Paignton	6933	Birtles Hall	84B	09.49	09.51	Origin not identified
084	—		Taunton-Minehead	4174		82D		09.54	
085	IC32	07.30	Paddington-Penzance	D861	Vigilant	83D	10.10	10.13	
086	IC62	07.35	Newport-Paignton	D7012		82A		10p18	
087	—		Yeovil-Taunton	4143		83B	10.32		
088	—		Castle Cary-Taunton	82044		83B	10.36		
089	IC60	07.50	Paddington-Paignton	D803	Albion	83D	10.42	10.47	
090	IC52	08.15	Paddington-Minehead	6856 4128	Stowe Grange	85A 83B	10.45	10.59	6856 replaced by 4128 at Taunton
091	IC25		Bristol-Penzance	D821	Greyhound	83D		10p53	
092	IC67		Paddington-Paignton	6953	Leighton Hall	81D		11p01	
093	—		Paddington-Minehead	5032 4143	Usk Castle	81A 83B	11.05	11.17	5032 replaced by 4143 at Taunton
094	ID20	08.06	Cardiff-Kingswear	D7009		82A		11p09	
095	IC26	08.30	Paddington-Falmouth	D818	Glory	83D		11p13	
096	IC68		-Kingswear	6903	Belmont Hall	86G		11p19	
097	IV25		Train not identified	5071	Spitfire	82B	11.25	11.28	Origin not identified
098	IC70	09.05	Paddington-Paignton	D856	Trojan	83D		11p31	Worked into Bristol by 45088 (21A) (probably a service from LMR)
099	IC64	06.35	Wolverhampton-Paignton	D7027		82A	11.32	11.35	
100	IV26	06.35	Walsall-Kingswear	D7002		82A	11.40	11.42	Worked into Bristol by 45659 (55A)
101	IC23	06.55	Wolverhampton-Penzance	D819	Goliath	83D	11.46	11.50	Worked into Bristol by 5089 (84A) via Bristol
102	IC59	07.45	Paddington-Paignton	D826	Jupiter	83A	11.54	11.57	
103	—		Taunton-Barnstaple	7326		83B		11.59	
104	IC29	09.30	Paddington-Perranporth & Newquay	D857	Undaunted	83D		12p01	
105	—		Taunton-Minehead	4110		83B		12.05	
106	IV27	06.40	Leicester-Paignton	D7013		82A	12.13	12.17	Worked into Bristol by 44814 (21A)

TABLE TWO (continued)

Train Ref. No.	Rep. No.	Time	Description	Motive power	Name	Allocation	Time		Remarks
							Arr.	Dep.	
107	—		Taunton-Exeter	5032	*Usk Castle*	81A		12.18	
108	IC73	10.05	Paddington-Kingswear	D829	*Magpie*	83A	12.36	12.40	
109	IC30	10.30	Paddington-Penzance	D1006	*Western Stalwart*	83D		12p55	Cornish Riviera Express
110	—	10.15	Paddington-Minehead	6026	*King John*	81A	13.11	13.25	
				6155		83B			6026 replaced by 6155 at Taunton
111	IC35		Carmarthen-Penzance	D822	*Hercules*	83D		13p14	
112	—		Paddington-Penzance	6021	*King Richard II*	81A	13.19	13.23	
113	IV31	07.43	Nottingham-Plymouth	D831	*Monarch*	83A	13.28	13.31	
114	IC76	08.50	Swansea-Minehead	4932	*Hatherton Hall*	83B	13.35	13.50	
				4103		83B			4932 replaced by 4103 at Taunton
115	—		Not identified	5046	*Earl of Cawdor*	84A		13p37	Possibly ex Paddington
116	IC75	09.05	Swansea-Kingswear	D7011		82A		13p42	
117	IC36		Treherbert-Paignton	4087	*Cardigan Castle*	83D		13p51	
118	IV33	08.00	Carmarthen-Penzance	D814	*Dragon*	83D		14p00	
119		08.00	Sheffield-Paignton	D7041		82A		14p07	
120	IC33	11.30	Paddington-Penzance	D842	*Royal Oak*	83A	14p10	14.16	Royal Duchy
121	—		Taunton-Ilfracombe	6327		83B			
122	—		Yeovil-Taunton	5563		83B	14.19	14.21	Departure E.C.S.
123	IV34		Not identified	6965	*Thirlestaine Hall*	83C	14.27	14.30	Probably ex-LMR
124	IC79	10.05	Wolverhampton-Kingswear	D7008		82A		14p33	
125	IC81	12.05	Paddington-Kingswear	D801	*Vanguard*	83D		14p35	Torbay Express
126	IC37	12.21	Cardiff-Newquay	D806	*Cambrian*	83D	14.50	14.54	
127	IV88	08.22	Manchester-Penzance	D840	*Resistance*	83A		14p59	
128	IC85	10.55	Wolverhampton-Minehead and Ilfracombe	D7016		82A	15.12	15.37	D7016 removed at Taunton
				4174		83B		15.45	For Minehead
				7337		83B			For Ilfracombe
129	—		Taunton-Minehead	4128		83B		15.24	
130	—	13.05	Paddington-Plymouth	7021	*Haverfordwest Castle*	81A	15.28	15.32	
131	IC84		Paddington-Kingswear	D851	*Temeraire*	83D		15p38	
132	IV89	08.45	Liverpool-Paignton	D7020		82A		15p42	
133	IV92	09.10	Manchester-Paignton	D866	*Zebra*	83D	15.54	15.58	
134	IV38	07.30	Newcastle-Paignton	D828	*Magnificent*	83A	16.01	16.06	
135	IV39	09.05	Bradford-Paignton	D7001		82A		16p11	Devonian

TABLE TWO (continued)

Train Ref. No.	Rep. No.	Time	Description	Motive power	Name	Allocation	Time Arr.	Dep.	Remarks
136	IC40	13.30	Paddington-Penzance	D830	*Majestic*	83A	16.17	16.21	
137	IV93	09.30	Liverpool-Plymouth	D850	*Swift*	83D	16.32	16.44	
138	—		Taunton-Minehead	4143		83B		16.39	
139	IC43	14.30	Paddington-Penzance	D848	*Sultan*	83A	16.55	17.03	
140	—		Bristol-Plymouth Parcels	3810		88A	17.01	17.26	
141	—		Taunton-Goodrington Sands	DMU				17.18	
142	IV42	09.20	Bradford-Paignton	D810	*Cockade*	83D	17.43	17.45	
143	—		Taunton-Barnstaple	7333		83B		17.57	
144	2		Bristol-Taunton	DMU			17.56	18.10	Departure E.C.S.
145	—		Taunton-Minehead	82044		83B		18.01	
146	—		Taunton-Exeter	4932	*Hatherton Hall*	83B		18.23	
147	—		Bristol-Taunton	DMU			18.46		
148	IV95	12.55	Manchester-Plymouth	D820	*Grenville*	83D	18.53	19.02	
149	IC45	16.30	Paddington-Truro	D841	*Roebuck*	83A	19.06	19.15	
150	3C06		Parcels	D817	*Foxhound*	83D	19.21		Departure not recorded

31

TABLE THREE

SURVEY POINT: TAUNTON – NORTHBOUND – DATE 27th JULY 1963

P = Passing time

Train Ref. No.	Rep. No.	Time*	Description	Motive power	Name	Allocation	Time Arr.	Time Dep.	Remarks
151	IF18	07.45	Newton Abbot-Porthcawl	DMU			09.33	09.37	
152	IN61	07.45	Paignton-Newcastle	D830	Majestic	83A	09.38	09.48	
153	IA27		Paignton-Paddington	D829	Magpie	83A	09.57		Trains 153 & 154 combined at Taunton hauled by D829
154	2C83		Minehead-Paddington	D6336		83A	10.02	10.15	
155	IM18	08.20	Paignton-Nottingham	D7000		82A	10.05	10.12	
156	IM20		Relief to Derby	D7047		82A	10.18	10.21	
157	IA36		Dartmouth-Paddington	D858	Valorous	83D	10p20		
158	IN48	09.00	Paignton-Sheffield	D7041		82A	10.30	10.35	
159	IM90		Exmouth-Manchester	D7068		81A	10.37	10.43	
160	IA41	06.45	Truro-Paddington	D1039	Western King	83D	10.44	10.50	
161	IM89	09.12	Paignton-Manchester	D825	Intrepid	83A	10p56		Devonian
162	IN37	09.00	Kingswear-Bradford	D869	Zest	83D	11p05		
163	—		Minehead-Manchester	6113		83B	11.08	11.19	Trains 163 & 164 combined at Taunton hauled by 4993 (83B)
164	IM14		Barnstaple-Manchester	6327		83B	11.11	11.19	
165	IM91	06.10	Penzance-Liverpool	D814	Dragon	83D	11p16		
166	IA47	09.45	Churston-Paddington	D816	Eclipse	83D	11p21		
167	—		Barnstaple-Taunton	7333		83B	11.43		
168	IA45	09.30	Plymouth-Paddington	D870	Zulu	83D	11p51		
169	3B	10.19	Newton Abbot-Bradford	D7053		82A	12.02	12.13	
170	IH22	10.05	Kingswear-Wolverhampton	D7070		82A	12p09		
171	IA52	11.15	Minehead-Paddington	D7011		82A	12.14	12.31	D7011 replaced by unidentified D70XX at Taunton
172	IF37	10.15	Paignton-Carmarthen	D7017		82A	12p15		
173	IX95		-Preston	D7003		82A	12.22	12.24	
174	IA51	11.10	Paignton-Paddington	D7052		82A	12p29		
175	—	08.00	Newquay-Manchester	D805	Benbow	83D	12p38		
176	IM93	10.45	Kingswear-Manchester	D7025		88A	12p47		
177	—	07.30	Penzance-Paddington	D807	Caradoc	83D	12.55	13.01	

TABLE THREE (continued)

Train Ref. No.	Rep. No.	Time*	Description	Motive power	Name	Allocation	Time Arr.	Time Dep.	Remarks
178	—		Barnstaple-Cardiff	7326		83B	12.58		Combined with train 184
179	IN86	08.43	Newquay-Newcastle	D835	*Pegasus*	83A		12p59	
180	IM23	11.35	Paignton-Nottingham	D7054		82A	13.07	13.11	
181	IA66	09.20	Dartmouth-Paddington	D842	*Royal Oak*	83A		13p11	
182	IA67		Falmouth-Paddington	D845	*Sprightly*	83A		13p39	
183	—		Ilfracombe-Wolverhampton	7337		83B	13.44		Combined with train 186
184	IT33	12.05	Minehead-Cardiff	82042		83B	13.58	14.07	Combined with train 178. 82042 replaced by 5963 (83B) at Taunton 82042 substitute for failure at Minehead
185	2C76		Exeter-Taunton	DMU			14.00		
186	2C83	12.45	Minehead-Wolverhampton	D6336		83A	14.17	14.31	Combined with train 183. D6336 replaced by 6904 (84C) at Taunton
187	IA72	12.32	Newton Abbot-Paddington	D7027		82A	14.24	14.27	
188	B2		Minehead-Taunton	DMU			14.30		
189	X702		Paignton-Cardiff	D7021		82A	14.31	14.35	
190	IA75	10.00	Newquay-Paddington	D852	*Tenacious*	83A		14p38	
191	IN68	09.05	Penzance-Bradford	D866	*Zebra*	83D	14.44	14.49	
192	—	09.45	Penzance-Paddington	D808	*Centaur*	83D		14p48	
193	IM97	13.28	Paignton-Manchester	D7019		82A	14.51	14.54	
194	IA83		Paignton-Paddington	D8XX		82A		14p53	Locomotive not identified
195	IE70		Paignton-Sheffield	D7069		83A	14.59	15.05	
196	IM96	10.05	Penzance-Manchester	D823	*Hermes*	82E	15.05	15.13	
197	—		Barnstaple-Taunton	41276			15.07	15.14	Departure E.C.S.
198	IA86	10.40	Penzance-Paddington	D8XX		83D		15p13	Locomotive not identified
199	IH34	11.20	Newquay-Wolverhampton	D810	*Cockade*	83B		15p26	
200	—	14.20	Minehead-Paddington	{9635 / 4143}		83B	15.37	15.47	Arrival double headed. Both locomotives replaced by unidentified D70XX
201	IA92	13.30	Kingswear-Paddington	D7067		81A		15p41	
202	IE24		Penzance-Sheffield	D800	*Sir Brian Robertson*	83D		15p47	
203	IA87	11.35	Newquay-York	D857	*Undaunted*	83D		15p57	
204	IF59	11.10	Penzance-Swansea	D820	*Grenville*	83A		16p16	
205	2B8		Minehead-Taunton	D7045		82A	16.19		

TABLE THREE (continued)

Train Ref. No.	Rep. No.	Time*	Description	Motive power	Name	Allocation	Time Arr.	Time Dep.	Remarks
206	IH33		Paignton-Birmingham	D7072		82A	16.26	16.30	
207	A41	12.30	Newquay-Paddington	D812	The Royal Naval Reserve 1859-1959			16p30	Via Bristol, locomotive and stock off train 205
208	A1	15.00	Paignton-Paddington	D811	Daring	83D		16p37	
209	—	16.42	Taunton-Paddington	D7045		82A		16.42	
210	IA12	11.50	Penzance-Paddington	D826	Jupiter	83D	16.52	16.57	
211	IH		Penzance-Wolverhampton	D839	Relentless	83A		17p05	
212	IM25		Paignton-Birmingham	D7016		82A	17.11	17.20	Departure E.C.S.
213	—		Minehead-Taunton	{D7011 / 6113}		82A / 83B	17.26	17.36	Double headed
214	—		Taunton-Weston-super-Mare	4904	Binnegar Hall	83B		17.34	
215	3C00		E.C.S.	D7018		82A	17.39		Departure not recorded
216	IT34	15.20	Kingswear-Cardiff	DMU			17.45	17.51	
217	—		Barnstaple-Taunton	6372		83B	17.47		
218	3A28	12.00	Penzance-Glasgow	D802	Formidable	83D	18.11	18.36	D802 failed at Taunton (fire) replaced by D7043
219	IA32	16.10	Kingswear-Paddington	D851	Temeraire	83A	18.25	18.34	
220	—	13.50	Penzance-Paddington	D806	Cambrian	83D	18.38	18.43	
221	2B94		Newton Abbot-Taunton	DMU			19.00		
222	B2		Taunton-Bristol	DMU				19.02	

* The 1963 working timetable was not available. Where the service was identical to that in 1962 the 1962 origin departure time is quoted.

TABLE FOUR

SURVEY POINT: TAUNTON – SOUTHBOUND – DATE 27th JULY 1963

P = Passing time

Train Ref. No.	Rep. No.	Time*	Description	Motive power	Name	Allocation	Arr.	Dep.	Remarks
223	IC22	06.30	Paddington-Penzance	D868	Zephyr	83D	09.31	09.34	
224	IC61		-Paignton	D7046		82A	09.33	09.47	
225	IC58	07.00	Paddington-Kingswear	D7067		81A	09p44		Origin not identified
226	—		Taunton-Minehead	D7011		82A		09.54	
227	IC62		Cardiff-Paignton	D7069		82A	10p00		
228	IC56		Paddington-Minehead	D7061		81A	10.18		
				D6336		83A		10.31	D6336 replaced D7061 at Taunton
229	IC25		Bristol-Penzance	D827	Kelly	83D	10p37		
230	—	07.50	Paddington-Paignton	D7060		81A	10.39	10.46	
231	IC63		Cardiff-Kingswear	DMU			10p45		
232	3A29	08.15	Paddington-Minehead	D7076		81A	10.46		4143 replaced D7076 at Taunton
				4143		83B		11.12	
233	IV25		Relief Walsall-Kingswear	D7073		82A	10.54	11.00	Train worked into Bristol by 45447 (21A)
234	IC66		-Paignton	D7019		82A	11.03	11.06	Origin not identified
235	C26	08.30	Paddington-Falmouth	D804	Avenger	83D	11p11		
236	IV26	06.35	Walsall-Kingswear	D7018		82A	11.17	11.22	Train worked into Bristol by 45617 Mauritius (21A)
237	—		Taunton-Barnstaple	6372		83B		11.25	
238	IB31	06.35	Wolverhampton-Paignton	D7072		82A	11.25	11.29	
239	IC23	06.55	Wolverhampton-Penzance	D836	Powerful	83A	11.32	11.40	
240	—	09.05	Paddington-Paignton	D811	Daring	83D	11p34		
241	B2		Taunton-Minehead	DMU				11.52	
242	IC59	07.45	Paddington-Paignton	D7016		82A	11.52	11.57	
243	IC29	09.30	Paddington-Newquay	D824	Highflyer	83A	11p56		via Bristol
244	—		Taunton-Exeter	D7061		81A		12.19	
245	IC73	10.05	Paddington-Kingswear	D851	Temeraire	83A	12.40	12.45	
246	2B		Bristol-Taunton	DMU			12.41	12.50	Departure E.C.S.
247	IC30	10.30	Paddington-Penzance	D828	Magnificent	83A	12p51		
248	IC72		Wolverhampton-Minehead and Barnstaple	D7045		82A	12.52	13.06	Arrival at Bristol behind 7019 (84A) 7333 took the Barnstaple portion D7045 worked forward to Minehead
				7333		83B		13.13	

TABLE FOUR (continued)

Train Ref. No.	Rep. No.	Time*	Description	Motive power	Name	Allocation	Arr.	Dep.	Remarks
249	IV27	06.40	Leicester-Paignton	D7051		82A	12.58	13.03	Arrival at Bristol behind 44666 (21A)
250	IC75	10.15	Swansea-Paignton	D7023		82A	13p16		
251	IC74		Paddington-Minehead	D7065		81A	13.16		D7011 replaced D7065 at Taunton
				D7011		82A		13.28	
252	IV31	07.43	Nottingham-Plymouth	D7000		82A	13.19	13.26	
253	IC76	08.50	Swansea-Minehead and Ilfracombe	D7043		82A	13.32		6113 replaced D7043 and worked to Minehead. 6327 took the Ilfracombe portion
				6113		83B		13.51	
				6327		83B		14.08	
254	IC78		Paddington-Paignton	D821	Greyhound	83D	13p32		
255	C36	08.00	Carmarthen-Penzance	D817	Foxhound	83D	13p55		
256	IC12	11.30	Paddington-Penzance	D1008	Western Harrier	81A	14p03		
257	—		E.C.S.	4591		83B	14.04	14.09	(ex Castle Cary?)
258	IV33	08.00	Sheffield-Penzance	D863	Warrior	83D	14.11	14.34	
259	IV34		Sheffield-Paignton	D7005		82A	14p21		
260	IC79	10.05	Wolverhampton-Kingswear	D7042		82A	14p31		
261	IC81	12.05	Paddington-Dartmouth	D854	Tiger	83D	14p36		
262	IC86		Cardiff-Newton Abbot	D869	Zest	83D	14.39	14.48	
263	IV88	08.22	Manchester-Penzance	D853	Thruster	83D	14p51		
264	—		Weston-super-Mare-Taunton	4932	Hatherton Hall	83B	15.15		
265	IC39		Paddington-Plymouth	D819	Goliath	83D	15.23	15.27	
266	IV89	08.45	Liverpool-Kingswear	D7041		82A	15p28		
267	4C9		Not identified	D7012		82A	15p33		
268	B2		Taunton-Minehead	DMU				15.33	
269	IV92	09.10	Manchester-Paignton	D864	Zambesi	83D	15.43	15.47	
270	IV93	09.30	Liverpool-Plymouth	D835	Pegasus	83A	15.52	15.59	
271	IC40	13.30	Paddington-Plymouth	D838	Rapid	83A	16.25	16.28	
272	—		Taunton-Barnstaple	7326		83B		16.31	
273	IV40	09.20	Bradford-Paignton	D7017		82A	16.34	16.45	
274	B2		Taunton-Minehead	DMU				16.49	
275	IC43	14.30	Paddington-Penzance	D829	Magpie	83A	17.02	17.06	
276	2C70		Taunton-Newton Abbot	DMU				17.15	
277	IV38	07.30	Newcastle-Paignton	D805	Benbow	83D	17.22	17.27	
278	IV39	09.05	Bradford-Paignton	D866	Zebra	83D	17.32	17.41	

TABLE FOUR (continued)

Train Ref. No.	Rep. No.	Time*	Description	Motive power	Name	Allocation	Time Arr.	Time Dep.	Remarks
279	—		Taunton-Barnstaple	7337		83B		17.58	
280	B2		Bristol-Taunton	DMU			18.08		
281	—		Parcels	4707		81C	18.21	18.29	
282	IC45	16.30	Paddington-Truro	D816	*Eclipse*	83D	19.07	19.11	

* The 1963 working timetable was not available. Where the service was identical to that in 1962 the 1962 origin departure time is quoted.

TABLE FIVE

SURVEY POINT: TAUNTON – NORTHBOUND – DATE 25th JULY 1964

P = Passing time

Train Ref. No.	Rep. No.	Time	Description	Motive power	Name	Allocation	Time Arr.	Time Dep.	Remarks
283	IF18	07.45	Newton Abbot-Swansea	DMU			09.22	09.30	
284	IN79	07.50	Paignton-Newcastle	D838	*Rapid*	83A	09.40	09.47	
285	IA25		Minehead-Paddington	D6329		83A	09.55		Trains 285 and 286 combined
286	—		Paignton-Paddington	D815	*Druid*	84A	09.58	10.09	headed by D815
287	IM18	08.20	Paignton-Nottingham	D7009		82A	10.05	10.11	
288	IM87	08.30	Paignton-Manchester	D7089		86A	10.13	10.17	
289	IA27		Kingswear-Paddington	D830	*Majestic*	83A		10p20	Departure E.C.S.
290	—		Ilfracombe-Taunton	6345		83B	10.23	10.33	Double headed
291	IN48	09.00	Paignton-Leeds	{D7055 / D7093}		82A	10.33	10.37	
292	IM90	09.18	Exmouth & Ilfracombe-Manchester	D7038		86A	10.40	10.53	Train 293 combined with 292 at Taunton headed by D7038
293	—			D6335		83A	10.41		
294	IA30		Plymouth-Paddington	D1019	*Western Challenger*	84A	10.46	10.49	
295	IM89	09.12	Paignton-Manchester	D802	*Formidable*	84A		10p55	
296	IN37	09.10	Kingswear-Bradford	D855	*Triumph*	84A	11.05	11.06	*Devonian*
297	IM91	06.10	Penzance-Manchester	D804	*Avenger*	84A		11p12	
298	IA34		Paignton-Paddington	D1039	*Western King*	87E		11p20	
299	—		Minehead-Taunton	4103		83B	11.27	11.35	Departure E.C.S.
300	—		Ilfracombe-Taunton	31406		83D	11.47		
301	IN40	10.20	Newton Abbot-Bradford	D845	*Sprightly*	83A	11.49	11.56	
302	IM34	10.10	Kingswear-Wolverhampton	D1033	*Western Trooper*	83A		11p53	
303	IA39		Minehead-Paddington	D7050		82A	11.59		D7063 replaced D7050 at Taunton
				D7063		81A	12.10		
304	IF30	10.25	Paignton-Carmarthen	D7044		82A		12p07	
305	IA42		Paignton-Paddington	D7045		82A		12p22	
306	IM95	08.00	Newquay-Manchester	D814	*Dragon*	84A		12p30	
307	IM93	10.45	Kingswear-Liverpool	D856	*Trojan*	84A		12p39	
308	IA48		Penzance-Paddington	D1029	*Western Legionnaire*	82A	12.47	12.52	
309	IT33		Ilfracombe and Minehead	7306		86E	12.58		Train 309 combined with 310 at Taunton headed by D7075
310	—		(12.05) - Cardiff	D7075		82A	13.17	13.30	
311	IN86	08.45	Newquay-Newcastle	D870	*Zulu*	84A		12p59	

TABLE FIVE (continued)

Train Ref. No.	Rep. No.	Time	Description	Motive power	Name	Allocation	Arr.	Dep.	Remarks
312	IM23	11.35	Paignton-Nottingham	D7052		82A	13.06	13.10	
313	IA52		Kingswear-Paddington	D816	Eclipse	84A	13p15		
314	IA58		Falmouth-Paddington	D1049	Western Monarch	84A	13p22		
315	IM35		Minehead and Ilfracombe-Wolverhampton	D6329		83A	13.45		Trains 315 and 316 combined at Taunton headed by D7004, D6329 from Ilfracombe, 7337 from Minehead
316	—			7337		83B	13.36		
317	IA59		Newton Abbot-Paddington	D7004		82A		13.58	
318	IT35	12.10	Paignton-Cardiff	D868	Zephyr	84A	14.18	14.21	
319	IA60		Newquay-Paddington	D7049		82A	14.24	14.30	
320	IE29	09.05	Penzance-Sheffield	D1071	Western Renown	84A		14p31	
321	IA62		Penzance-Paddington	D843	Sharpshooter	83A	14.40	14.43	
322	B2	14.45	Penzance-Paddington	D1005	Western Venturer	84A		14p45	
323	2C77		Taunton-Bristol	DMU				14.49	
324	—		Exeter-Taunton	DMU		83B	15.00	15.07	Departure E.C.S.
325	IM92		Ilfracombe-Taunton -Preston	7303		84A	15.01	15.09	
326	B2		Minehead-Taunton	DMU			15.07	15.11	
327	IA64		Paignton-Paddington	D1003	Western Pioneer	82A	15.08	15.17	
328	IE70	13.00	Paignton-Sheffield	D7010		82A	15p15		
329	IM96	10.50	Penzance-Manchester	D823	Hermes	83A	15.22	15.25	
330	IA75		Penzance-Paddington	D811	Daring	84A	15.29	15.38	
331	IH34	11.20	Newquay-Wolverhampton	D842	Royal Oak	83A	15.41	15.45	
332	IA70		Kingswear-Paddington	D1051	Western Ambassador	84A		15p46	
333	IE24	11.00	Penzance-Sheffield	D819	Goliath	84A		15p53	Cornishman
334	IN87	11.45	Newquay-York	D844	Spartan	83A		15p58	
335	2C89		Minehead-Paddington	D7067		81A		16p15	
336	IF59	11.20	Penzance-Swansea	D809	Champion	84A	16.17	16.42	
337	IM36	14.30	Paignton-Wolverhampton	D7017		82A		16p22	
338	IA78		Newquay-Paddington	D1015	Western Champion	84A	16.34	16.36	
339	2C83		Minehead-Taunton	D7050		82A		16p39	Departure E.C.S.
340	IA82		Paignton-Paddington	D821	Greyhound	84A	16.43	16.47	
341	IA84		Penzance-Paddington	D1041	Western Prince	82A		16p50	
342	IM39	12.20	Penzance-Wolverhampton	D824	Highflyer	83A	17.06	17.10	
343	IM25	15.20	Paignton-Birmingham	D7056		81A	17.16	17.30	

TABLE FIVE (continued)

Train Ref. No.	Rep. No.	Time	Description	Motive power	Name	Allocation	Time Arr.	Dep.	Remarks
344	—		Barnstaple-Taunton	6363		83B	17.38		
345	IT44	15.21	Kingswear-Cardiff	DMU			17.41	17.50	
346	3Z55		E.C.S.	{ D6344 } { D7022 }		84A 82A	17.53	18.30	D7022 & D6344 double headed, D7022 having failed. Both replaced by D7038 at Taunton
				D7038					
347	IM99	13.15	Penzance-Glasgow	D818	Glory	84A	18.15	18.19	

TABLE SIX

SURVEY POINT: TAUNTON – SOUTHBOUND – DATE 25th JULY 1964

Train Ref. No.	Rep. No.	Time	Description	Motive power	Name	Allocation	Time		Remarks
							Arr.	Dep.	
348	IC19	07.00	Swindon-Penzance	D805	Benbow	84A	09.19	09.23	
349	—		Paddington-Kingswear	D1051	Western Ambassador	84A		09p40	
350			Taunton-Minehead	D7050		82A		09.44	
351	IC24	07.50	Cardiff-Paignton	D7010		82A		09p59	
352	IC26		Paddington-Penzance	D1015	Western Champion	84A	10.05	10.10	
353	—		Taunton-Minehead	D7075		82A		10.16	
354	IC28	09.40	Bristol-Penzance	D844	Spartan	83A	10p29		
355	IC30		Paddington-Paignton	D7056		81A	10.34	10.42	
356	IC35	08.05	Kingswear-Cardiff	DMU				10p36	
357	IV59	Relief	Wolverhampton-Dartmouth	D7058		81A		10p47	
358	IC38		Paddington-Minehead	D7063		81A	10.51		D6329 replaced D7063 at Taunton
				D6329		83A		11.02	
359	IC40	Relief	Paddington-Paignton	D1041	Western Prince	82A	10p58		
360	IV25	Relief	Walsall-Kingswear	D7022		82A	11.05	11.08	Train worked into Bristol by 44777 (2E)
361	IV26	07.32	Birmingham-Paignton	D7015		82A	11.20	11.23	Train worked into Bristol by 45674 (2E)
362	—		Taunton-Ilfracombe	6363		83B		11.26	
363	IV51		Wolverhampton-Dartmouth	D7017	Hermes	82A	11.30	11.38	
364	IC43		Paddington-Newquay	D823		83A		11p30	
365	IC45		Paddington-	D1010	Western Campaigner	84A		11p55	Destination not identified
366	IV52	08.00	Wolverhampton-Penzance	D7047		82A	12.08	12.12	Train worked into Bristol by 7011 (85A)
367	B2		Taunton-Minehead	DMU				12.16	
368	IC77		Taunton-Ilfracombe	D6335		83A		12.17	
369	2B	10.30	Bristol-Taunton	DMU			12.29	12.32	Departure E.C.S.
370	IV27	06.26	Leicester-Paignton	D7046		82A	12.35	12.40	Train worked into Bristol by 45267 (15A)
371	IC48		Paddington-Kingswear	D7092		82A	12.35	12.41	
372	IC51		Paddington-Penzance	D1056	Western Sultan	87E		12p50	
373	IC55		Paddington-Minehead	D7067		81A	13.00	13.08	

TABLE SIX (continued)

Train Ref. No.	Rep. No.	Time	Description	Motive power	Name	Allocation	Arr.	Dep.	Remarks
374	IC58	07.50	Llanelli-Minehead and Ilfracombe	D7004		82A	13.11		D7050 took over from D7004 on the Minehead portion, 31406 worked to Ilfracombe
				D7050		82A		13.23	
				31406		83D		13.31	
375	IC53	10.45	Cardiff-Kingswear	D7013		82A		13p19	
376	IC61		Paddington-Paignton	D7076		81A		13p28	
377	IC63	Relief	Relief to Paignton	D1752		83D		13p34	
378	IV33	08.10	Sheffield-Penzance	D838	Rapid	83A		13p41	
379	—	07.43	Nottingham-Plymouth	D802	Formidable	84A	13.47	13.50	
380	IC64	08.00	Carmarthen-Penzance	D7089		82A		13p52	
381	IC6-		Paddington-Penzance	D854	Tiger	84A		13p58	Cornishman
382	IV42	Relief	Sheffield-Paignton	D7024		82A	13.58	14.05	
383	IV34	08.15	Sheffield-Paignton	D7009		82A		14p15	
384	IV54	10.05	Wolverhampton-Paignton	D7018		82A		14p27	
385	—	12.20	Cardiff-Newton Abbot	DMU			14.33	14.50	
386	IC70		Paddington-Paignton	D7090		86A		14p34	
387	IC75		Paddington-Plymouth	D849	Superb	83A	14.51	15.08	
388	IV88	08.20	Manchester-Penzance	D804	Avenger	84A		14p56	
389	IV89	08.45	Liverpool-Kingswear	D1033	Western Trooper	83A		15p15	
390	IC77		Paddington-	D1042	Western Princess	86A		15p27	Destination not established
391	B2		Taunton-Minehead	DMU				15.38	
392	IV92	09.05	Manchester-Paignton	D870	Zulu	84A	15.41	15.47	
393	IV93	09.20	Liverpool-Plymouth	D856	Trojan	84A	15.56	16.00	
394	IV38	07.30	Newcastle-Paignton	D814	Dragon	84A	16.06	16.12	
395	IC80		Paddington-Penzance	D1031	Western Rifleman	83A	16.15	16.23	
396	—		Taunton-Barnstaple	7306		86E		16.24	
397	IV40	09.05	Bradford-Paignton	D7055		82A	16.37	16.45	
398	IC83		Paddington-Kingswear	D1023	Western Fusilier	86A	16.52	16.59	
399	3C04		Parcels	D855	Triumph	84A	17.05	17.31	
400	2C77		Taunton-Goodrington Sands	DMU				17.12	
401	IV39	10.35	Bradford-Paignton	D843	Sharpshooter	83A	17.28	17.34	Devonian
402	—		Taunton-Barnstaple	7337		83B		17.45	
403	—		Taunton-Minehead	D7021		82A		18.06	
404	IV95	12.25	Manchester-Plymouth	D844	Spartan	83A	19.10		Departure not recorded

TABLE SEVEN

SURVEY POINT: TAUNTON – NORTHBOUND – DATE 21st AUGUST 1965

P = Passing time

Train Ref. No.	Rep. No.	Time	Description	Motive power	Name	Allocation	Time Arr.	Time Dep.	Remarks
405	1F18	07.00	Plymouth-Swansea	D1044	Western Duchess	84A	09.16	09.25	
406	1N79	07.30	Paignton-Newcastle	D852	Tenacious	83A	09.39	09.43	
407	1A26	08.05	Paignton & Minehead-Paddington	D7096		82A	09.49	10.05	D7096 worked forward trains 407 & 408 combined
408	2C83		Paddington	D7003		82A	09.51		
409	1M18	08.20	Paignton-Nottingham	D7008		82A	10.03	10.08	
410	1M87	08.30	Paignton-Manchester	D7048		82A	10.12	10.16	
411	—	07.55	Ilfracombe-Manchester	D6331		83A	10.13		Trains 411 & 412 combined at
412	1M90	09.18	Exmouth- Manchester	D7038		84A	10.40	10.46	Taunton going forward with D7038
413	2C84		Minehead-Taunton	DMU			10.17		
414	1A27	08.20	Kingswear-Paddington	D864	Zambesi	83A	10p19		
415	1N48	09.00	Paignton-Leeds	D7046		82A	10.33	10.36	
416	1A28	06.00	Penzance-Paddington	D1068		82A	10.48	10.53	
417	2C83	09.50	Minehead-Taunton	D6347		84A	10.52	11.03	Departure E.C.S.
418	1M89	09.12	Paignton-Manchester	D847	Strongbow	83A	10p58		
419	1A31	08.15	Ilfracombe-Paddington	D7090		84A	11p08		
420	1N37	09.10	Kingswear-Bradford	D803	Albion	84A	11p14		
421	1M91	06.30	Penzance-Manchester	D1004	Western Crusader	84A	11p23		
422	1A3–	10.25	Minehead-Paddington	D7039		84A	11.30	11.38	
423	1A33	10.00	Paignton-Paddington	D815	Druid	84A	11p30		
424	—	09.25	Ilfracombe-Taunton	DMU			11.37	11.44	Departure E.C.S.
425	1N40	10.20	Newton Abbot-Bradford	D7009		82A	11.50	11.56	
426	1F30	10.25	Paignton-Carmarthen	D7016		82A	12.00	12.09	
427	1M34	10.05	Paignton-Wolverhampton	D855	Triumph	83A	12p05		
428	1A42	11.00	Paignton-Paddington	D7045		82A	12p35		
429	1M95	08.00	Newquay-Manchester	D1031	Western Rifleman	84A	12p45		
430	1M93	10.45	Kingswear-Manchester	D1019	Western Challenger	84A	12p53		
431	—	10.20	Ilfracombe-Cardiff	D6333		83A	12.56		Combined with 433
432	1A48	07.45	Penzance-Paddington	D1036	Western Emperor	81A	13.03	13.06	
433	2C33	12.17	Minehead-Cardiff	D7002		82A	13.06	13.29	Trains 431 & 433 combined at Taunton and worked forward by D7002
434	1N86	08.45	Newquay-Newcastle	D844	Spartan	83A	13p14		

TABLE SEVEN (continued)

Train Ref. No.	Rep. No.	Time	Description	Motive power	Name	Allocation	Arr.	Dep.	Remarks
435	1M23	11.35	Paignton-Nottingham	D1009	Western Invader	84A	13.20	13.36	
436	1A48	11.20	Dartmouth-Paddington	D854	Tiger	83A		13p33	
437	1M35	11.10	Ilfracombe-Wolverhampton	D6348		84A	13.33		Trains 437 & 438 combined at Taunton going forward behind D7087
438	2C33	12.40	Minehead-Wolverhampton	D7020		82A	13.42		
				D7087		82A		13.54	
439	1A52	12.45	Ilfracombe-Paddington	D1003	Western Pioneer	84A		13p42	
440	1A59	12.32	Newton Abbot-Paddington	D7092		84A	13.53	13.59	
441	1M96	08.55	Penzance-Manchester	D1072	Western Glory	81A	13.57	14.10	
442	1A60	10.05	Newquay-Paddington	D1005	Western Venturer	84A		14p06	
443	1N87	09.20	Penzance-York	D828	Magnificent	84A	14.18	14.24	
444	2C84	11.45	Ilfracombe-Taunton	DMU			14.20		
445	1A62	10.00	Penzance-Paddington	D1041	Western Prince	82A		14p27	
446	Z29		L.E.	D7077		82A		14p33	
447	1A64	13.28	Paignton-Paddington	D859	Vanquisher	83A		14p51	
448	1E70	13.00	Paignton-Sheffield	D7099		84A	14.58	15.06	
449	1A75	10.30	Penzance-Paddington	D850	Swift	83A	15.07	15.48	
450	1T35	13.50	Paignton-Cardiff	D7024		82A	15.14	15.16	
451	1M54	11.20	Penzance-Wolverhampton	D853	Thruster	83A		15p23	
452	1A70	13.30	Kingswear-Paddington	D7063		81A		15p41	
453	2C83		Minehead-Taunton	D6347		82A	15.43	15.47	Departure E.C.S.
454	1N21	11.00	Penzance-Bradford	D807	Caradoc	84A		15p51	
455	1N45	11.45	Newquay-York	D813	Diadem	84A		15p58	
456	1F59	11.30	Penzance-Swansea	D842	Royal Oak	83A		16p11	
457	1M36	14.30	Paignton-Wolverhampton	D851	Temeraire	83A	16.21	16.31	
458	2C83	15.15	Minehead-Taunton	D7003		82A	16.24	16.32	
459	1A78	12.30	Newquay-Paddington	D1XXX				16p27	Locomotive not identified
460	1A82	15.00	Paignton-Paddington	D1046	Western Marquis	84A		16p35	
461	2C83	15.45	Minehead-Taunton	D7065		81A	16.48		
462	1A84	12.00	Penzance-Paddington	D1071	Western Renown	82A	16.51	16.59	
463	1M39	12.30	Penzance-Wolverhampton	D837	Ramillies	83A		17p05	
464	1A90	14.45	Ilfracombe-Paddington	D7080		81A		17p22	
465	2B97	17.30	Taunton-Weston-super-Mare	D841	Roebuck	83A		17.31	
466	2C84	15.10	Ilfracombe-Taunton	DMU			17.38		

TABLE SEVEN (continued)

Train Ref. No.	Rep. No.	Time	Description	Motive power	Name	Allocation	Time Arr.	Time Dep.	Remarks
467	1T45	15.20	Kingswear-Cardiff	D7083		86A	17.41	17.50	
468	1M99	13.05	Penzance-Liverpool	D1032	*Western Marksman*	84A	18.14	18.17	

TABLE EIGHT

SURVEY POINT: TAUNTON – SOUTHBOUND – DATE 21st AUGUST 1965

Train Ref. No.	Rep. No.	Time	Description	Motive power	Name	Allocation	Time Arr.	Dep.	Remarks
469	2C83	09.10	Taunton-Minehead	D7039		84A		09.10	
470	IC19	07.00	Swindon-Penzance	D823	Hermes	84A	09.15	09.18	
471	IC22	07.05	Paddington-Dartmouth	D7063		81A		09p45	
472	IC24	07.55	Cardiff-Paignton	D7024		82A		10p01	Train arrived in Bristol behind D7029 (86A)
473	IC26	07.30	Paddington-Penzance	D1047	Western Lord	84A	10.04	10.10	
474	2C83	10.15	Taunton-Minehead	D7002		82A		10.15	
475	IC28	09.35	Bristol-Penzance	D813	Diadem	84A		10p23	
476	IC32	08.15	Paddington-Ilfracombe	D829	Magpie	84A		10p34	
477	IC30	07.50	Paddington-Paignton	D851	Temeraire	83A	10.44	10.48	
478	IB64	08.05	Cardiff-Kingswear	D7083		86A	10.53	11.00	
479	IC40	08.30	Paddington-Falmouth	D1071	Western Renown	82A		10p55	
480	2C83	10.50	Taunton-Minehead	D7020		82A		10.55	
481	IV51	06.35	Wolverhampton-Paignton	D7017		82A	11.03	11.08	Train arrived in Bristol behind D1725 (82A)
482	IC43	09.05	Paddington-Paignton	D1046	Western Marquis	84A	11p19		
483	2C87	11.20	Taunton-Ilfracombe	DMU				11.22	
484	IV52	06.58	Wolverhampton-Penzance	D7098		84A	11.33	11.42	Train arrived in Bristol behind 45006 (2B)
485	—	10.26	Bristol-Taunton	DMU			11.47	11.51	Departure E.C.S.
486	IV27	06.55	Leicester-Paignton	D7094		82A	11.55	12.12	Train arrived in Bristol behind D88 (ML)
487	IC45	09.30	Paddington-Newquay	D1033	Western Trooper	84A	11p59		
488	IC47	09.50	Paddington-Minehead	D7065		81A	12.20		D7086 replaced D7065 at Taunton, however D7086 returned LE 30 mins. later. D7065 departed LE presumably to take over the train
				D7086		84A		12.27	
489	IC48	10.05	Paddington-Kingswear	D835	Pegasus	83A	12.31	12.39	
490	IC58	08.10	Llanelli-Penzance	D839	Relentless	83A	12.34	12.53	
491	IC50	10.15	Paddington-Ilfracombe	D7077		82A		12p44	
492	IC51	10.30	Paddington-Penzance	D1039	Western King	84A		12p51	

TABLE EIGHT (continued)

Train Ref. No.	Rep. No.	Time	Description	Motive power	Name	Allocation	Time Arr.	Time Dep.	Remarks
493	IV53	08.00	Wolverhampton-Ilfracombe and Minehead	D7012		82A	12.56		Train arrived in Bristol behind 7908 (2A)
				D6331		83A		13.14	D6331 replaced D7012 and worked the Ilfracombe portion.
494	IC55	08.00	Carmarthen-Paignton	D6347		84A		13.21	D6347 took the Minehead portion
495	IC57	10.55	Paddington-Kingswear	D7075		82A	13p09		
				D7072		81A	13p14		
496	IC59	10.50	Cardiff-Ilfracombe and Minehead	D7052		82A	13.21		D6333 replaced D7052 and worked the Ilfracombe portion. D7003 worked to Minehead
				D6333		83A		13.35	
				D7003		82A		13.42	
497	IV32	07.53	Nottingham-Paignton	D1044	Western Duchess	84A	13p26		
498	IV33	07.02	Bradford-Penzance	D852	Tenacious	83A	13p37		
499	IV88	08.20	Manchester-Paignton	D7048		82A	13p47		
500	IC67	11.05	Paddington-Ilfracombe	D1029	Western Legionnaire	82A	13p53		
501	IV34	08.52	Sheffield-Paignton	D7008		82A	14p00		
502	IX98		Relief from Birmingham	D1025	Western Guardsman	86A	14.15	14.17	
503	IV54	10.05	Wolverhampton-Kingswear	D70XX			14p29		Locomotive not identified
504	IC70	11.30	Paddington-Penzance	D7093		82A	14p29		
505	IV89	08.45	Liverpool-Plymouth	D847	Strongbow	83A	14p42		
506	IC75	12.05	Paddington-Penzance	D1062	Western Courier	87E	14.49	15.02	
507	IV92	09.05	Manchester-Penzance	D1004	Western Crusader	84A		15p06	
508	IV93	09.20	Liverpool-Paignton	D803	Albion	84A	15.15	15.23	D7052 added as pilot from Taunton
509	IC77	12.30	Paddington-Plymouth	D7064		81A	15.22	15.25	
510	IC78	09.40	Carmarthen-Taunton	D7038		84A	15.30	15.36	
511	IV37	07.30	Newcastle-Paignton	D7009		82A	15.38	15.44	
512	2C83	15.40	Taunton-Minehead	DMU				15.47	
513	2C84	16.00	Taunton-Ilfracombe	DMU				16.02	Departure E.C.S.
514	IC80	13.30	Paddington-Penzance	D1057	Western Chieftain	87E	16.08	16.12	
515	IV39	10.05	Bradford-Paignton	D844	Spartan	83A	16.13	16.18	
516	IV40	09.00	Bradford-Paignton	D7037		84A	16.38	16.52	
517	IC83	14.00	Paddington-Penzance	D864	Zambesi	83A	16.43	16.48	
518	—	16.52	Taunton-Minehead	DMU				16.52	
519	IV95	12.58	Manchester-Plymouth	D828	Magnificent	84A	18.10	18.14	

5. Services through the Severn Tunnel 1962-1965

In addition to those trains already discussed which passed through Taunton en route to South Wales or the North West additional traffic flows to be considered on this route are the services to Paddington, the South coast via Westbury and also local trains on the Bristol route. The observer for the first year of recording travelled only to Patchway but in subsequent years went on to Severn Tunnel Junction so for 1963 onwards the services from South Wales to Gloucester and beyond are also included. Interestingly a survey was also carried out at Patchway in 1961 although the observer did not arrive on site until nearly midday, the date of the survey being Saturday, 5th August. In that year, all services except Bristol locals were in the hands of steam traction, the locals being diesel multiple units. Observations lasted seven hours and during that period four Kings were noted on Paddington services. Although the Britannias were still allocated to Cardiff Canton only two were seen and one of these was on a North and West service. Most other Paddington services were in the hands of Castles with cross country services having a mixture of Castles, Halls and Granges. A feature of services here was the use of Standard Cl.9F 2-10-0s on passenger work, five being recorded on that occasion. Two parcels trains and four goods were also noted.

SEVERN TUNNEL JUNCTION: Britannias were the mainstay of services from South Wales in the late 1950s but were among the first victims of dieselisation being transferred to the Midland Region. They were replaced briefly by surplus Castles and Kings before the arrival of the Hymeks. This photo predates the introduction of the standardised headcode system when the Western was using individual 3-digit numbers to identify its trains. Several of the Western Region Britannias could continue to be easily identified when transferred away by the type of handholds on the smoke deflectors, these being modified following the 1956 Didcot accident involving 70026 *Polar Star*. In this view 70016 *Ariel* heads the 13.55 Paddington-Pembroke Dock at Badminton. 13th June 1959. *(Hugh Ballantyne)*

1962– Services from Taunton

The trends in train services on this route have already been discussed, therefore comment is only made on the motive power situation.

The first locomotive hauled service, following the DMU worked Newton Abbot-Swansea was train *008* for Cardiff with a Didcot based Hall (note the duplication of reporting number with train *526*), then came the Exeter-Manchester (a Banbury based Hall) and the Ilfracombe and Minehead to Manchester which despite its fourteen coaches had nothing larger than a Grange from St. Philips Marsh. (*013* and *016* retained their Warship power throughout). An Old Oak Castle headed *025* Paignton-Carmarthen whilst *028* and *029* had similar power.

The combined Minehead and Barnstaple to Cardiff was in the care of a St Philips Marsh Hall followed by a similarly allocated County worked *046* to Manchester. Warship hauled *052* was followed by a Neath Castle on *061* to Swansea with a Pontypool Road Hall on *068* and a further St. Philips Grange on *072*, both to Cardiff. *073* for Glasgow actually exchanged Warships at Bristol for the run up the North and West route.

1962 Services to Taunton

Opening the action Eastbound on the Cardiff-Kingswear was the Old Oak Castle which returned on *025*, followed by the Swansea-Minehead (the Hall returning with the Northbound service). The Swansea-Kingswear was provided with a Modified Hall and the Carmarthen-Penzance had the return engine for *061*. A stranger for 1962 was a Bath Road Hymek in charge of the Cardiff-Newquay whilst *127* (Manchester-Penzance) was a through Warship working. The following Liverpool-Paignton was the outward turn for the County returning on *046* but *133* was another Warship turn. The Pontypool Road Hall on *137* Liverpool-Plymouth was obviously not on good form being a rare case for assistance through the tunnel, this being provided by 2-6-2 tank 6115. The final Southbound service from Manchester (*148*) was also headed by a Warship.

1963 Services from Taunton

Motive power for the trains that operated in 1963 followed the 1962 pattern until the Paignton-Carmarthen service, other than a Hall working the Ilfracombe and Minehead service in place of a Grange.

The Carmarthen service was this time in the hands of a Western which resorted to the services of a 2-6-2 tank for assistance through the tunnel. *173* extra to Preston was provided with a Hall from Westbury depot. Both of the following Manchester trains were also worked by Halls, the former with a 41XX pilot through the tunnel. The Minehead and Ilfracombe to Cardiff service went over to diesel power with a Cardiff Hymek whilst the train originating at Paignton was headed by a Cl.9F from Cardiff East Dock. *193* (Paignton-Manchester) this time had an Old Oak Modified Hall but Penzance-Swansea (*204*) was downgraded from Castle to Hall traction. Unfortunately 1M99 – the Glasgow service – was not seen on this occasion – the Warship on this service had to be replaced at Taunton following a fire and it is doubtful if the substitute Hymek worked through.

1963 Services to Taunton

The Western noted above worked East to Bristol on the Swansea-Minehead/Ilfracombe service whilst the Hymek on the return journey of this train went out on *250* Swansea-Paignton. The Cl.9F noted above, went to Bristol on *255* Carmarthen-Penzance whilst *262* to Newton Abbot was headed by a Bath Road Hymek. *266* Liverpool-Kingswear, provided work for a St. Philip's Marsh Castle whilst *270* Liverpool-Plymouth with an Oxford Hall needed assistance from 4156 through the tunnel. Warships worked through as in 1962.

1964 Services from Taunton

Banbury shed provided the Hall for *288* Paignton-Manchester in 1964 though the Exmouth-Manchester (now with an Ilfracombe portion) had super power with Brush Type 4 D1743. Similar power was provided for the Manchester trains *295* and *297*, however the Brush on the latter service took assistance from a 41XX tank. Another Brush was in charge of Paignton-Carmarthen (*304*) and *306* (Newquay-Manchester) was similarly powered. The Ilfracombe and Minehead-Cardiff service produced a Western and *318*, also to Cardiff, a Canton Hymek.

The final Penzance-Swansea also was Brush powered and so in one year all turns except one had seen both steam and Warships ousted from the route.

1964 Services to Taunton
The Northbound pattern was repeated, *380* (Carmarthen-Penzance) was Hymek worked and *761,* Carmarthen-Taunton, had a Western. No steam was recorded and so other than the DMU turns all other duties were performed by Brush Type 4s.

1965 Services from Taunton
With the demise of DMUs on the first train (Plymouth-Swansea) a Hymek worked the leg from Bristol. The following Paignton-Manchester *(410)* was of note as the Brush (D1777) was allocated to Tinsley at that time. All trains then, up to and including 10.45 Kingswear-Manchester *(430)* were also Brush worked though a Hymek was provided for the Ilfracombe/Minehead - Manchester train, thereafter it was Brush Type 4s all the way.

1965 Services to Taunton
Brush supremacy was broken only twice – on both occasions by English Electric Type 3s with D6897 (Landore) on train *507* (Manchester-Penzance) and D6936 (Canton) on 17.38 Cardiff-Plymouth.

1962 Paddington Services from South Wales
By 1962 Hymeks had just established themselves on these duties and handled all trains unless stated otherwise. Services recorded (in order) originated at Fishguard Harbour, Swansea, Treherbert (Modified Hall), Cardiff (Castle), Carmarthen, Pembroke Dock, Fishguard (Castle), Neyland, Milford Haven (Castle), Milford Haven, Pembroke Dock and Neyland.

Going into Wales trains ran to Pembroke Dock (two), Neyland (Castle), Swansea, Pembroke Dock (two), Swansea, Pembroke Dock, Fishguard, Treherbert (Modified Hall), Fishguard Harbour, Swansea and Neyland (Modified Hall).

Previous incumbents of the task had been Castles based at both Landore (Swansea) and Cardiff, the latter being replaced by the Britannias. These in turn gave way to a small

number of Kings whilst some Castles also came back to Cardiff when the Britannias moved on. All these services worked to London via Chipping Sodbury to Swindon.

1963 – South Wales to Paddington
The first up train noted in 1963 (at Severn Tunnel Junction) originated from Swansea with a Hymek. The source of the next service was not established but was worked by a Cardiff East Dock Castle. The following Carmarthen train was headed by a Western, a Hymek was on the Pembroke train and a Modified Hall worked from Neyland. The next pair of trains originating again at Pembroke Dock and Neyland were both in the hands of Hymeks whilst a Western followed on a Milford Haven service. The final Pembroke and Swansea trains were also Western worked. There were no Treherbert trains.

Westbound the first six trains were all in the hands of Westerns, and it was after 14.00 before a Hymek appeared on a Swansea duty. Thereafter four Westerns and two Hymeks were responsible for the services with no steam duties.

1964 – South Wales to Paddington
The first Swansea service was headed by a Western. This was followed by a relief headed by a Brush Type 4 as were the next two trains (from Swansea). A further relief was entrusted to a Western as were all the other Paddington trains for the day. Ten trains ran compared to thirteen in 1962.

Westbound services divided between Westerns (seven) and Brush Type 4s (three) except for a similarly timed service to Swansea as seen in 1963 which was again Hymek worked.

1965 – South Wales to Paddington
Services were as follows – Swansea (Brush), Cardiff (Hymek), Swansea (two – both Brush), Pembroke Dock (Brush), Swansea (Western), Pembroke Dock (Brush), Swansea (two – both Westerns). Only nine trains were noted on this occasion but the survey was taken one month later.

A new motive power combination was seen on the first Westbound train with a Hymek/Western double header on a Fishguard service. A second Fishguard train was Brush worked thence Swansea (Western),

Pembroke Dock (Hymek), Swansea (two – both Brush), Swansea (Hymek) and Swansea (Brush).

South Coast via Westbury and/or Bristol services

These services included many Saturday-only trains and as such attracted much 'stand-in' motive power.

1962 saw an interesting group of trains starting with train *558* Blaina-Weston-super-Mare with Grange 6852 *Headbourne Grange* (82B) followed by Swansea-Weston-super-Mare, being a DMU. Train *561* (Cardiff-Portsmouth) produced a Cl.9F and Treherbert-Weymouth, a Hall. Cardiff-Pokesdown, Cardiff-Portsmouth (trains *563/6*), a Treherbert-Portsmouth *(568)* and a second Cardiff-Portsmouth *(569)* were all Hall worked. Then followed Swansea-Brockenhurst, Carmarthen-Weston-super-

Mare and Cardiff-Brighton (train *576*) which continued the supply of Halls. Modernisation intervened with two DMU workings to Bristol.

A Porthcawl to Weston service was headed by 2-6-0 6319 before a final Cardiff-Portsmouth which was double-headed, again by Halls. Finally two further Bristol services were worked by DMUs. In addition, six freights were noted, worked respectively by County 1011 *County of Chester,* 7249 + 4152, 7250, 3836 + 4152, 6800 *Arlington Grange* + 4119 and 5213 + 6158.

Going into Wales the day started with a degree of uncertainty with an unidentified seven coach service headed by a Grange (train *525*). Then followed a Weston-super-Mare - Swansea, Castle hauled and train *531* (Bournemouth-Cardiff) with a Hall. Another unidentified train bound for Swansea was also seen – probably IV05, 08-48 ex-New Milton, in view of the motive power (a Westbury Hall). A

SEVERN TUNNEL JUNCTION: For Saturday cross country services engines and stock came from all sources. On Saturday 28th July 1962. Hall 4943 *Marrington Hall* of Pontypool Road shed is seen at the head of 09.32 Cardiff-Pokesdown service (train *563*). The photograph was taken as the train approached Bath having been recorded as passing Patchway at 10.30. It would probably have been around 11.10 at this point, the train having avoided Bristol Temple Meads by taking the North to East curve at Dr Days Junction. The stock appears to be a mixture of LMS and GWR designs with possibly a couple of BR Mark Is in the middle. The service remained steam operated in 1963 but the corresponding 1964 train was Hymek worked.

(Hugh Ballantyne)

further Portsmouth-Cardiff (Hall) was followed by a DMU local before IA42 came through with a Castle. It is probable that this train originated at Paddington. Certainly another South coast service bound for Cardiff was IV08 (Hall) before the only Manor appeared (train *540*) again unidentified but probably 10.00 Brighton-Cardiff. A Bristol-Cardiff DMU preceded train *543*, Portsmouth-Cardiff (Cl.9F) and the Brighton-Cardiff (Hall). A further Hall was rostered for Weymouth-Cardiff, then followed a local DMU and finally another Hall on Weymouth Quay-Cardiff. Only one freight was noted, headed by Bath Green Park Cl.9F 92007.

1963 Bristol and Weymouth Services

The survey for this and subsequent years was carried out at Severn Tunnel Junction.

The previous year's Blaina-Weston service appeared to have been replaced by a Hymek hauled Cardiff-Bristol. this was not seen at Severn Tunnel Junction due to the later start time. A DMU worked the Swansea-Weston-super-Mare with Halls on the next three South coast services. A Hymek appeared on the following Cardiff-Portsmouth but in view of the reporting number carried (7A38) it may have been a substitute for other motive power. A Modified Hall was on the Swansea-Brockenhurst but the Carmarthen-Weston-super-Mare rated a Castle. Cardiff-Portsmouth was hauled by a Grange but the Brighton service was in the hands of a Hymek. Two Cardiff-Bristol trains were DMUs whilst the final Portsmouth train was double headed by a Hymek and a Hall. The remaining Bristol trains were again DMU worked.

Freights noted on this route were headed by 2895 + 5191, 5978 *Bodinnick Hall* + 6140, 92003, 5977 *Beckford Hall,* D1019 *Western Challenger* (Margam-Old Oak Common), 5213 (total six).

Westbound the first train noted was Bristol-Liverpool which was Warship worked. Train *607* Bournemouth-Cardiff was headed by a Grange whilst the Bournemouth-Swansea had Hall power, as did Weston-Swansea *(601)* and Paignton-Manchester. Train *613* (Portsmouth-Cardiff) was a Hymek and similar service (train *617*) was entrusted to a Hall as was train *621.* In between a Tyseley Hall appeared on an

unidentified Carmarthen service (*614*). Brighton-Cardiff power was as outwards whilst Weymouth-Cardiff produced a DMU. Bristol-Cardiff was a Hymek. A final Bristol-Cardiff came through with an Oxford based Hall at its head. The only freight was handled by 5978 + 5191.

1964 – Bristol and Weymouth Services

The Swansea-Weston DMU again opened proceedings, but was followed by a Brush Type 4 on Cardiff-Portsmouth. A relief Cardiff-Bournemouth had a Hall but the main train was hauled by a Hymek as was Cardiff-Portsmouth. Llanelli-Brockenhurst however brought out a Neath Grange. Thereafter, *1061* Cardiff-Portsmouth was again a Hymek with two Bristol services DMU worked. A final Cardiff-Portsmouth produced a further Hymek with a DMU on Swansea-Bristol. There was a marked decrease in the service level provided two years earlier. Freight activity was represented by 6876 *Kingsland Grange,* 3859 + 4137, 3844 + 4115, D1046 *Western Marquis,* 3810 + 4144, 6847 *Tidmarsh Grange,* 7226 – an increase of one.

One passenger service which could not be explained was that at 14.53 when Carlisle-based Stanier Cl.5 45061 assisted by 2-6-2 tank 4121 worked through the tunnel but the train was not seen at Bristol or East thereof. Possibly the train worked to Swindon and on to the Great Central route from there.

Coming into Wales the Bristol-Liverpool had lost its Warship of 1963 in favour of a Brush Type 4. A Hall was still in charge of Bournemouth-Cardiff but a Western headed the Swansea service. The relief Portsmouth-Cardiff was also handled by a Hall with a Hymek on the main train. Following Portsmouth trains were Hymek worked. Bristol-Cardiff DMUs continued but a tea-time service was provided with a Hymek. Still later, the next Bristol train arrived with a Brush Type 4 whilst the final Portsmouth-Cardiff was Hymek worked.

A mid-afternoon freight was in the hands of a Brush Type 4.

1965 – Bristol & Weymouth Services

A further marked reduction in services was notable (although the later survey date will have

SEVERN TUNNEL JUNCTION. A scene that tended to disappear rather than be dieselised, long freight trains, frequently loose coupled and unbraked. 2-6-2 tank 4137 pilots 2-8-0 3848 as they set off from the yard at Severn Tunnel Junction, Eastwards for the long slog up to Patchway. 5th June 1961. *(B. W. L. Brooksbank)*

had some influence). All services were DMU worked except Llanelli-Bournemouth which was hauled by a Brush Type 4 and the final Cardiff-Plymouth service was an EE Type 3.

Freight - 92226 worked a twelve wagon service in the early afternoon followed by D6926 + D7041 and D6902 + D6904 whilst ECS was handled by D1697 and a milk train by D1053 *Western Patriarch.*

Westbound Taunton-Swansea and Bristol-Liverpool were Brush Type 4 worked were train *815* 09.28 Portsmouth-Cardiff and 1024 (10.29 service between these stations) whilst 13.08 Portsmouth-Cardiff had a Hymek. Otherwise DMUs ruled supreme.

A Cl.9F from Banbury appeared on a mid morning freight being the only one recorded.

Gloucester Line Services

As noted earlier the survey point was moved in 1963 to Severn Tunnel Junction and thus for 1963-1965 activity on the Gloucester line could also be recorded (see Chapter 6) as well as the comings and goings at the adjacent engine shed.

1963

Firstly there was the local Chepstow-Newport/Cardiff service which was DMU worked – three trains were recorded in each direction.

Other East to North services were Swansea-Newcastle and Cardiff-Leeds both Hymeks, Swansea/Cardiff-Cheltenham (DMU) and Cardiff-Birmingham the afternoon train *(688)* being a through working of LMR Metro Cammell units. Steam also appeared on a Cardiff-Cheltenham (63XX), Cardiff-Birmingham and Pembroke-Derby (both Halls).

Freight traffic – D1041 *Western Prince* worked a through freight late in the afternoon Northbound. Other freights taking the Gloucester line at STJ but not reaching the observer North of Gloucester were hauled by 6993 *Arthog Hall,* 3839, 3856, D7086 (Parcels), 92233, 92236, 6975 *Capesthorne Hall,* 92217 and 6320. The only stranger in the light engine movements was 2251 of Bristol Barrow Road.

Westbound services in addition to those

The midweek 16.18 Gloucester-Cardiff DMU service worked by a Swindon-built 3-car cross country set. These distinctive units were some of the first casualties of mainstream withdrawals, many of their Derby and MCW built counterparts surviving into the 1990s. Grange Court Junction, 8th June 1963. *(R. E. Toop)*

locals mentioned above comprised DMUs on Cheltenham-Cardiff/Swansea services, the outward working of the LMR DMU mentioned above from Nottingham, a Hymek on Derby-Pembroke, 63XX on one Cheltenham-Cardiff diagram, a Castle on an LMR or NER originating through service to Cardiff (*620*), a Hymek on *623* Newcastle-Cardiff and also one on unidentified train *637*.

Freight services saw 2231, 92208 and a parcels with 6987 *Shervington Hall*. A light engine of note was Stanier Cl.8F 48110 from Shrewsbury.

1964

DMU services to Chepstow and Cheltenham were as in 1963. IM28, Cardiff-Newcastle went through with a Western in charge and the Pembroke Dock-Derby was Hymek worked whilst Cardiff-Leeds also had a Hymek.

Freight traffic started with 7318 which worked through to be seen at Gloucester. D1603 also was at work as were 44811, 6863 *Dolhywell Grange*, 3818 and 6864 *Dymock Grange*. The parcels service was again Hymek

worked. Light engine movements included the passage of an English Electric Type 3 to the shed.

In the opposite direction the Derby-Pembroke was Hymek worked, and the Nottingham-Cardiff a DMU. The Western noted above returned with the afternoon Newcastle-Cardiff (*724*). 73024 worked down an hour later with another portion. (This locomotive had worked train *724* into Gloucester from the North!). Finally Leeds-Cardiff came through with a Hymek in charge.

Freight activity was in the hands of 3700, D1596 (through from Gloucester), 2231, 48680 (also through from Gloucester) 3838 and a parcels with D7034. Light engines included Annesley Cl.8F 48368, D1605 and D6915.

1965

Upgrading was the game for 1965 with a Hymek being introduced on a Cardiff-Gloucester diagram and the Derby-Pembroke Dock going up to a Brush Type 4 as did the Cardiff-York, whilst the afternoon Cardiff-

SEVERN TUNNEL JUNCTION. Perhaps not received with great enthusiasm by the observer on the South Wales line at the time were the "car carriers" which ran through the Severn Tunnel in the days before the Severn road bridge was built. This was the typical formation until the final survey in 1965 when the duty went over to a Class 37. In this view, taken on 5th June 1961, 2-6-2 tank 6125 is in charge.

(B. W. L. Brooksbank)

Sheffield was worked by a Peak.

Freight work was in the hands of 92203, 7029 *Clun Castle,* 48060, D7051, D1012 *Western Firebrand,* D1756 and 44715. The riddle of the disappearing Carlisle Cl.5 continued with 44900 being noted on a four coach ECS working which escaped further recording. Passenger traffic from the North mirrored that in the other direction in terms of motive power. Freight duties were performed by D1070 *Western Gauntlet,* 4671, D1721 and 5235.

One working which has not so far been mentioned but which took place every two to three hours was the Pilning to Severn Tunnel Junction car carrier, this service being provided in the days before the construction of the Severn Bridge allowing Bristol motorists to avoid the long drive via Gloucester to cross the River Severn.

This train was worked in 1962-4 by 41XX tanks but in the final year had an EE Type 3 at its head. Thus all steam was eliminated from passenger workings at this location for the final season. One working that was noted on the final survey was D6972 on train *822* which consisted of four 41XX tanks which presumably were being towed away for scrap on this date.

TABLE NINE

SURVEY POINT: PATCHWAY – WESTBOUND – 28th JULY 1962

P = Passing time

Train Ref. No.	Rep. No.	Time	Description	Motive power	Name	Allocation	Arr.	Dep.	Remarks
520			Freight	92007		82F		09p38	
521		09.35	Bristol-Cardiff	DMU				09p52	
522	Z59		Train not identified	D7038		88A		09p54	
523	IX96		Relief Paignton-Preston	6836	Estevarney Grange	86G		10p23	Train worked to Bristol by 5075 (88A)
524	IF11	07.55	Paddington-Pembroke Dock	D7034		88A		10p28	
525			Train not identified	6822	Manton Grange	88A		10p41	
526	IT25	09.55	Weston-super-Mare (Locking Road) - Porthcawl	6319		82B		10p52	
527			Weston-super-Mare-Swansea	5092	Tresco Abbey	88A		11p04	
528	IF15	08.55	Paddington-Pembroke Dock	D7037		88A		11p12	
529	IM97		Bristol-Huncote	4968	Shotton Hall	82B		11p20	Probable that this is actually IM87 07.30 Paignton-Manchester
001	2C70	07.45	Newton Abbot-Swansea	DMU				11p24	
008	IT25	08.33	Paignton-Cardiff	4994	Downton Hall	81E		11p52	
530	IM89	09.55	Paddington-Neyland	5050	Earl of St.Germans	82B		12p17	
013	IM90	09.12	Paignton-Manchester	D849	Superb	83A		12p23	
011	IV14	10.00	Exeter-Manchester	6991	Acton Burnell Hall	84C		12p27	
531	IF24	09.00	Bournemouth-Cardiff	5999	Wollaton Hall	82D		12p31	
532	IM91	10.35	Paddington-Swansea	D7035		88A		12p38	
016		06.10	Penzance-Liverpool -Swansea	D825	Intrepid	83A		12p49	
533				4933	Himley Hall	82D		13p05	Possibly IV05 08.48 ex New Milton. Origin not confirmed.
015	IM14	08.35	Ilfracombe & Minehead-Manchester	6834	Dummer Grange	82B		13p15	
534	IF27	10.55	Paddington-Pembroke Dock	D7033		88A		13p18	
535	IV07	09.27	Portsmouth-Cardiff	4914	Cranmore Hall	82B		13p30	
536			Bristol-Severn Branch?	DMU				13p32	
537	IA42		Service not identified	5096	Bridgwater Castle	88A		14p13	
025	IF30	10.15	Paignton-Carmarthen	5042	Winchester Castle	81A		14p19	
028	IM95	08.00	Newquay-Manchester	5081	Lockheed Hudson	81A		14p25	
538	I-32	11.55	Paddington-Pembroke Dock	D7010		88A		14p33	

TABLE NINE (continued)

Train Ref. No.	Rep. No.	Time	Description	Motive power	Name	Allocation	Time Arr.	Dep.	Remarks
539	IV08	10.34	Portsmouth-Cardiff	6909	*Frewin Hall*	88A		14p36	Probably 10 a.m. Brighton-Cardiff
540	IC90			7805	*Broome Manor*	88A		14p40	
029	IM93	10.45	Kingswear-Manchester	4096	*Highclere Castle*	81A		14p42	
541		13.58	Weston-super-Mare-Cardiff	DMU				14p54	
542	IF41	12.55	Paddington-Swansea	D7039		88A		15p08	
543	IV10	11.37	Portsmouth-Cardiff	92237		88A		15p30	
033	IT35	12.05	Minehead & Barnstaple-Cardiff	6919	*Tylney Hall*	82B		15p44	
544	IV11	11.00	Brighton-Cardiff	4918	*Dartington Hall*	88A		15p51	
545			L.E.	4152		86E		16p02	
046	IM97	12.00	Kingswear-Manchester	1028	*County of Warwick*	82B		16p20	
546	IF45	13.55	Paddington-Pembroke Dock	D7036		88A		16p27	
052	IM96	10.05	Penzance-Manchester	D823	*Hermes*	83D		16p53	
547	IF46	14.55	Paddington-Fishguard Harbour	D7025		88A		16p55	
548		13.45	Weymouth-Cardiff	4942	*Maindy Hall*	82B		17p06	
549	2702	17.00	Bristol-Cardiff	D7007		82A		17p23	
550			Paddington-Treherbert	7919	*Runter Hall*	81D		17p37	
551	IF54	17.35	Paddington-Fishguard	D7024		88A		17p45	
061	IF59	11.10	Penzance-Swansea	5062	*Earl of Shaftesbury*	87A		17p52	
552	2		Bristol-Pilning	DMU				17p56	
553	IF55	17.55	Paddington-Swansea	D7037		88A		18p22	
554			Paddington-Neyland	7925	*Westol Hall*	88A		18p37	
068	IT41	12.42	Newquay-Cardiff	6905	*Claughton Hall*	86G		18p59	
555	IT43	16.15	Weymouth Quay-Cardiff	4909	*Blakesley Hall*	82D		19p32	
073	IM99	12.00	Penzance-Glasgow	D827	*Kelly*	83A		19p35	
072	IT45	15.20	Kingswear-Cardiff	6852	*Headbourne Grange*	82B		19p48	

PATCHWAY: 92220 *Evening Star* approaches Patchway station with summer Saturday service 10.30 Cardiff-Portsmouth (see train *569*). The use of Cl.9Fs on Saturday extras was widespread. However the exploits of 92220 on the prestigious weekdays Red Dragon service from South Wales to London are well documented elsewhere. *(John L. Champion)*

PATCHWAY: This view was taken after the end of the 1962 summer timetable. Reporting number 061 was then used for a combined 12.50 Cardiff-Brighton and Portsmouth whereas on 28th July 1962 the train was the 13.00 Cardiff-Brighton (train *576*). 6808 *Beenham Grange*, 29th September 1962. *(Peter W. Gray)*

TABLE TEN

SURVEY POINT: PATCHWAY – EASTBOUND – 28th JULY 1962

P = Passing time

Train Ref. No.	Rep. No.	Time	Description	Name	Motive power	Allocation	Arr.	Dep.	Remarks
094	C63	08.06	Cardiff-Kingswear	*Winchester Castle*	5042	81A		9p19	
557	IA18	04.55	Fishguard-Paddington		D7025	88A		9p24	
558	IB01	06.55	Blaina-Weston-super-Mare	*Headbourne Grange*	6852	82B		9p30	
559	B		Swansea-Weston-super-Mare (Locking Road)		DMU			9p56	
560	IA26	07.30	Swansea-Paddington		D7036	88A		10p03	
561	052	09.06	Cardiff-Portsmouth		92237	88A		10p13	
562	E336		Treherbert-Weymouth	*Burwarton Hall*	6932	88A		10p24	
563	055	09.32	Cardiff-Pokesdown	*Marrington Hall*	4943	86G		10p30	
564	A32		Treherbert-Paddington	*Burton Agnes Hall*	6998	81A		10p39	
565			Cardiff-Paddington	*Tintern Abbey*	5087	87A		10p50	
566	056	10.06	Cardiff-Portsmouth	*Maindy Hall*	4942	82B		11p02	
567	IA35	07.20	Carmarthen-Paddington		D7024	88A		11p07	Red Dragon
568	057		Treherbert-Portsmouth	*Kinlet Hall*	4936	88A		11p14	
569	058	10.30	Cardiff-Portsmouth	*Breccles Hall*	6936	88A		11p39	
114	IC76	08.50	Swansea-Minehead	*Tylney Hall*	6919	82B		11p48	
116	IC75	09.05	Swansea-Kingswear	*Hart Hall*	7907	82B		11p55	
570	IA53	06.40	Pembroke Dock-Paddington		D7037	88A		12p02	
117			Treherbert-Paignton	*Cardigan Castle*	4087	83D		12p10	
118	IC36	08.00	Carmarthen-Penzance	*Earl of Shaftesbury*	5062	87A		12p18	
571		09.55	Swansea-Brockenhurst	*Helmster Hall*	6912	88A		12p31	
572			Fishgaurd-Paddington	*Brecon Castle*	5023	82C		12p40	
573	IA58	08.00	Neyland-Paddington		D7028	88A		12p50	
574		02.30	Stockport-Bristol Parcels	*County of Chester*	1011	82B		13p26	Passed through Bristol T.M. 14.05
126	IC37	12.21	Cardiff-Newquay		D7007	82A		13p33	
127	IV88	08.22	Manchester-Penzance	*Resistance*	D840	83A		13p38	
575	IB11	09.45	Carmarthen-Weston-super-Mare	*Claughton Hall*	6905	87A		13p48	
132	IV89	08.45	Liverpool-Paignton	*County of Warwick*	1028	82B		14p01	
576	061	13.00	Cardiff-Brighton	*Blakesley Hall*	4909	82D		14p09	
133	IV92	09.10	Manchester-Paignton	*Zebra*	D866	83D		14p15	

Train Ref. No.	Rep. No.	Time	Description	Motive power	Name	Allocation	Time Arr.	Dep.	Remarks
577	2		Pilning-Bristol	DMU				14p29	
137	IV93	09.30	Liverpool-Plymouth	6958	*Oxburgh Hall*	86G		15p06	Assisted by 6115 (86G)
578	IA87	14.06	Cardiff-Bristol	DMU				15p15	
579		09.53	Pembroke Dock-Paddington	D7022		88A		15p26	Assisted by 4152 (86E)
580			Freight	7249		86E		15p37	
581	A90	11.00	Milford Haven-Paddington	5001	*Llandovery Castle*	81A		15p54	
582			Freight	7250		86E		16p14	
583		14.10	Porthcawl-Bristol	6319		82B		16p18	
584	IA05	12.05	Milford Haven-Paddington	D7034		88A		16p52	Assisted by 4152 (86E)
585			Freight	3836		86E		17p08	
586		16.25	Cardiff-Portsmouth	{5984 / 5999}	*Linden Hall* / *Wollaton Hall*	84B / 82D		17p24	
148	IV95	12.55	Manchester-Plymouth	D820	*Grenville*	83D		17p29	
587	IA20	13.05	Pembroke Dock-Paddington	D7032		88A		17p52	Assisted by 4119 (86E)
588		17.30	Freight	6800	*Arlington Grange*	86A		18p17	
589			Cardiff-Bristol	DMU				18p45	
590			Pilning-Bristol	DMU				19p36	
591	IA44	14.40	Neyland-Paddington	D7035		88A		19p53	Assisted by 6158 (86E)
592			Freight	5213		86A		19p58	

TABLE ELEVEN

SURVEY POINT: PATCHWAY – WESTBOUND – 27th JULY 1963

P = Passing time

Train Ref. No.	Rep. No.	Time*	Description	Motive power	Name	Allocation	Arr.	Dep.	Remarks
593			Chepstow-Newport	DMU			09.22	09.29	
594			Bristol-Liverpool	D860	Victorious	83D		09p26	Assisted by 5191 (86E)
595			Freight	5978	Bodinnick Hall	82B		09p47	
596			Cheltenham-Cardiff	DMU			09.50	09.52	
597			Bristol-Cardiff	DMU			10.18	10.20	
598	Z28	07.55	Paddington-Swansea	D1015	Western Champion	81A		10p53	
599			Pilning-S.T.J. Car Carrier	4150		86E	11.02		
600	IF19		Weston-super-Mare-Swansea	5990	Dorford Hall	84C	11.12	11.15	
601	IM87		Paignton-Manchester	6922	Burton Hall	89A	11.21	11.38	Train worked to Bristol by D7005/23 (Both 82A)
602	IV69		Derby-Pembroke Dock	D7033		88A		11p38	
603	IF15	08.55	Paddington-Swansea	D1018	Western Buccaneer	88A		11p40	
151	IF18	07.45	Newton Abbot-Portcawl	DMU				11p44	
604			Cheltenham-Cardiff	6381		85B	11.46	11.50	
605	IF20	09.55	Paddington-Carmarthen	D1037	Western Empress	88A		12p25	
606		10.35	Paddington-Swansea	D1058	Western Nobleman	82A		12p38	
161	IM89	09.12	Paignton-Manchester	D825	Intrepid	83A		12p40	
159	IM90		Exmouth-Manchester	6915	Mursley Hall	89A		12p45	
607	V04	09.00	Bournemouth-Cardiff	6821	Leaton Grange	86G		12p53	
608	IF15		Paddington-Swansea	D1038	Western Sovereign	88A		13p00	
165	IM91	06.10	Penzance-Liverpool	D814	Dragon	83D		13p07	
609			Chepstow-Newport	DMU			13.10	13.11	
610	V05		Bournemouth-Swansea	5967	Bickmarsh Hall	81A	13.19	13.21	
611	IF27	10.55	Paddington-Swansea	D1044	Western Duchess	88A		13p27	
612	IV71		Nottingham-Cardiff	DMU			13.29	13.35	
164	IM14		Minehead & Barnstaple-Manchester	5948	Siddington Hall	86G	13.36	13.37	
613	IV07	09.27	Portsmouth-Cardiff	D7083		88A	13.42	13.46	
614			-Carmarthen	7929	Wyke Hall	84E		13p52	Point of origin not established
173	IX95		-Preston	5929	Hanham Hall	82D		14p02	
172	IF37	10.15	Paignton-Carmarthen	D1046	Western Marquis	88A	14.18	14.23	Assisting engine 6114 (861) detached at S.T.J.

61

TABLE ELEVEN (continued)

Train Ref. No.	Rep. No.	Time	*Description	Motive power	Name	Allocation	Arr.	Dep.	Remarks
615	1·2	11.55	Paddington-Swansea	D7031		88A		14p26	
616			Freight	2231		88A		14p31	
175	IM93	08.00	Newquay-Manchester	6912	Helmster Hall	88A		14p36	Assisted by 4128 (86E)
176	V08	10.45	Kingswear-Manchester	6901	Arley Hall	86G		14p46	
617	B2	10.34	Portsmouth-Cardiff	6917	Oldlands Hall	84B	14.53	14.55	
618			Weston-super-Mare-Cardiff	DMU			15.10	15.15	
619	IF41	12.55	Paddington-Swansea	D1012	Western Firebrand	88A		15p21	Train noted at Gloucester. Loco changed there
620	IV60		-Cardiff	5081	Lockheed Hudson	88L		15p26	
621	V10	11.37	Portsmouth-Cardiff	6950	Kingsthorpe Hall	88L		15p40	
622	OZ52		Light Engine	D1054	Western Governor	88A	15.41	15.50	Loco to Depot – also seen at Gloucester
623	IV70	08.10	Newcastle-Cardiff	D7034		88A		15p59	Engines changed at Gloucester
624	IV11	11.00	Brighton-Cardiff	D7087		?		16p01	
189	X702		Paignton-Cardiff	92232		88L		16p16	
625		12.05	-Severn Tunnel Junction	DMU			16.19		Arrived via Gloucester line
184	IT33		Minehead & Ilfracombe-Cardiff	D7030		88A		16p24	
193	IM97		Paignton-Manchester	6966	Witchingham Hall	81A		16p34	
626			Freight	92208		88A		16p35	Also seen at Gloucester
627	IF45	13.55	Paddington-Neyland	D7038		88A	16.38	16.44	
628	2		-Severn Tunnel Junction	DMU		–	16.50		Arrived via Gloucester line
196	IM96	10.05	Penzance-Manchester	D823	Hermes	83A		17p02	
629	IF46	14.55	Paddington-Fishguard	D1062	Western Courier	88A		17p10	
630		13.45	Weymouth-Cardiff	DMU				17p17	
631			Cheltenham-Cardiff	DMU			17.22	17.27	
632			Pilning-Severn Tunnel Junction Car Carrier	4144		86E			
633	2T02	17.00	Bristol-Cardiff	D7049		82A	17.39		
204	IF59	11.10	Penzance-Swansea	5961	Toynbee Hall	87A	17.40	17.48	
634	IM66		Birmingham-Fishguard	73068		85C		17p54	Train not recorded at Gloucester
635	IF54	17.35	Paddington-Fishguard	D1043	Western Duke	88A	18p02	18p04	

TABLE ELEVEN (continued)

Train Ref. No.	Rep. No.	Time*	Description	Motive power	Name	Allocation	Time Arr.	Dep.	Remarks
636	IF55	17.55	Paddington-Fishguard	D7057		81A		18p27	
637	IV69		Train not identified	D7033		88A		18p37	Train noted at Gloucester. Locomotive changed at Gloucester
638			Chepstow-Cardiff	DMU			18.48	18.50	
639			Transfer Freight	D3103		86E		18p58	
640			Parcels	6987	Shervington Hall	88L		19p00	
641			Bristol-Cardiff	6910	Gossington Hall	81F	19.03	19.07	
642	2		Unidentified Service	DMU			19.27		Arrival from Gloucester line

• The 1963 Working Timetable was not available. Where the service was identical to that in 1962 the 1962 origin departure time is quoted.

TABLE TWELVE

SURVEY POINT: SEVERN TUNNEL JUNCTION – EASTBOUND – 27th JULY 1963

P = Passing time

Train Ref. No.	Rep. No.	Time*	Description	Name	Motive power	Allocation	Arr.	Dep.	Remarks
643		06.55	Swansea-Weston-super-Mare		DMU		09.20	09.26	
644	IA26	07.30	Swansea-Paddington		D7038	88A	09.34	09.35	
645	052	09.06	Cardiff-Portsmouth	Kingsthorpe Hall	6950	88L	09.45	09.49	
646	N28		Swansea-Newcastle		D7028	82A		09p53	
647		09.26	Cardiff-Birmingham		DMU		10.01	10.20	
648	055	09.32	Cardiff-Bournemouth	Rydal Hall	6986	82C	10.09	10.16	
649	IA34		–Paddington	Earl of Mount Edgecombe	5043	88L		10p30	
650		07.35	Carmarthen-Paddington	Western Duke	D1043	88A		10p35	
651	056	10.06	Cardiff-Portsmouth	Thirlestaine Hall	6965	86A		10p45	
652	IM31	10.15	Cardiff-Birmingham Snow Hill	Shervington Hall	6987	85A		11p00	
653	7A38	10.30	Cardiff-Portsmouth		D7008	82A	11.08	11.20	
253	IC76	08.50	Swansea-Minehead & Ilfracombe	Western Marquis	D1046	88A		11p35	
250	IC75		Swansea-Paignton		D7038	88A		11p39	
654	IA53	06.40	Pembroke Dock-Paddington		D7057	88A		11p47	
655			Freight		92232	85B		11p51	Gloucester route
255	C36	08.00	Carmarthen-Penzance	Arthog Hall	6993	88L		12p00	
656	2		Newport-Chepstow		DMU		12.05	12.09	
657		09.55	Swansea-Brockenhurst	Little Wyrley Hall	7913	88A	12.13	12.16	
658		08.00	Neyland-Paddington	Witherslack Hall	6990	81A		12p22	
659	IM72	08.30	Pembroke-Derby	Claughton Hall	6905	87A		12p48	
660		12.15	Cardiff-Cheltenham		DMU		12.56	13.00	
262	IC86		Cardiff-Newton Abbot		D7049	82A		13p04	
263	IV88	08.22	Manchester-Penzance	Thruster	D853	83D		13p09	
661	B11	09.45	Carmarthen-Weston-super-Mare	Elmley Castle	7003	85B	13.17	13.19	
662	060		Cardiff-Portsmouth	Yiewsley Grange	6859	88L		13p22	
663	1061	13.00	Cardiff-Brighton		D7015	82A		13p39	
266	IV89	08.45	Liverpool-Kingswear	Cardigan Castle	4087	82B		13p44	

TABLE TWELVE (continued)

Train Ref. No.	Rep. No.	Time*	Description	Name	Motive power	Allocation	Arr.	Dep.	Remarks
269	IV92	09.10	Manchester-Paignton	Zambesi	D864	83D	13.49	13.51	Gloucester line
664			Freight		3839	88J		13p54	Gloucester line
665			Freight		3856	88A	13.58	14.02	Gloucester line
270	IV93	09.30	Liverpool-Plymouth	Gossington Hall	6910	81F		14p15	Assisted by 4156 (86E)
666		12.00	Swansea-Cheltenham		DMU		14.17	14.23	
667	4E71		Freight	Western Prince	D1041	88A		14p31	via Gloucester
668	IA87	09.53	Pembroke Dock-Paddington		D7050	82A		14p35	
669		14.06	Cardiff-Bristol		DMU		14.45	14.59	
670			Freight		2895	88L	14.46	14.48	Tunnel Route. Assisted by 5191 (86E)
671	IN61		Cardiff-Leeds		D7033	88A		14p52	
672	2		Train not identified		DMU		15.17	15.34	Gloucester route
673	3A24		Parcels		D7086	88A	15.27	15.31	Gloucester route
674	2B78		Cardiff-Bristol		DMU		15.41	15.43	
675			Severn Tunnel Junc.-Bristol W. Freight Depot	Bodinnick Hall	5978	82B		15p57	Assisted by 6140 (86E)
676			Freight		92003	88A		16p04	Tunnel Route
677		15.30	Cardiff-Cheltenham		6381	85B	16.09	16.10	
678			Freight	Beckford Hall	5977	81D		16p10	Tunnel Route
679			Freight		92233	88A		16p28	Gloucester Route
680	IA90		Neyland-Paddington		D7036	88A		16p40	
681	IA05	12.05	Milford Haven-Paddington	Western Champion	D1015	81A		16p44	
682	1065	16.25	Cardiff-Portsmouth	Bickmarsh Hall	5967	81A	16.59	17.01	
					D7083	88A			
683	IV95	12.55	Manchester-Plymouth	Steadfast	D846	83A		17p07	Train appeared to be delayed–had not reached Taunton by 19.00
684			Severn Tunnel Junction-Chepstow		DMU			17.07	
685			Swansea-Chepstow		DMU		17.23	17.25	
686	IA20	13.05	Pembroke Dock-Paddington	Western Ranger	D1013	81A		17p36	
687			Freight		92236	88L		17p38	
688	IM28		Cardiff-Birmingham		DMU			17p46	Gloucester route
689			Carmarthen-Bristol		DMU		18.05	18.09	
690	2H86		Cardiff-Cheltenham		D7034	88A	18.23	18.26	

TABLE TWELVE (continued)

Train Ref. No.	Rep. No.	Time*	Description	Motive power	Name	Allocation	Time Arr.	Time Dep.	Remarks
691			Severn Tunnel Junc.-Pilning Car Carrier	4144		86E		18.28	
692	6A81		Freight. Margam-Old Oak Common	D1019	Western Challenger	81A		18p57	Tunnel route
693			Freight	5213		86A		19p05	Tunnel route
694			Freight	6975	Capesthorne Hall	87A		19p05	Gloucester route
695			Freight	92217		84C		19p13	Gloucester route
696			Freight	6320		86E		19p25	Gloucester route
697	IA44		Swansea-Paddington	D1044	Western Duchess	88A		19p35	
698			Cardiff-Bristol	DMU			19.42	19.45	

• The 1963 Working Timetable was not available. Where the service was identical to that in 1962 the 1962 origin departure time is quoted.

TABLE THIRTEEN

SURVEY POINT: SEVERN TUNNEL JUNCTION – WESTBOUND – 25th JULY 1964

Train Ref. No.	Rep. No.	Time	Description	Motive power	Name	Allocation	Time Arr.	Time Dep.	Remarks
699	IM84		Bristol-Liverpool	D1595		?		09p30	
700			Cheltenham-Cardiff	DMU			09.51	09.53	
701			Bristol-Cardiff	DMU			10.07	10.08	
702	2		Chepstow-Newport	DMU			10.29	10.30	
703	IF11		Paddington-Fishguard Harbour	D1045	*Western Viscount*	86A		10p39	
704			Pilning-Severn Tunnel Junc. Car Carrier	4121		86E	10.52		
705	IF13		Paddington-Pembroke Dock	D1026	*Western Centurion*	86A		10p58	
706	IF15		Paddington-Swansea	D1038	*Western Sovereign*	86A		11p05	
707	IF19		Weston-super-Mare-Swansea	D7016		82A	11.16	11.18	
708	IV69		Derby-Pembroke Dock	D7066		86A		11p19	
709			Cheltenham-Cardiff	DMU			11.37	11.43	
283	IF18	07.45	Newton Abbot-Swansea	DMU				12p02	
288	IM87	08.30	Paignton-Manchester	6911	*Holker Hall*	2D		12p10	
710	IF20		Paddington-Pembroke Dock	D1052	*Western Viceroy*	86A		12p17	
295	IM89	09.12	Paignton-Manchester	D1600		?		12p32	
292	IM90	09.18	Exmouth & Ilfracombe-Manchester	D1743		?		12p39	
711			Freight	3700		86E	12.47		From Gloucester line
712			Bournemouth-Cardiff	6947	*Helmingham Hall*	85B		12p47	Assisted by 4156 (86E)
713			Chepstow-Newport	DMU			13.07	13.16	
297	IM91	06.10	Penzance-Manchester	D1722		82A	13.20	13.23	
714	IA46		Bournemouth-Swansea	D1048	*Western Lady*	86A		13p22	
715	IF27		Paddington-Swansea	D1070	*Western Gauntlet*	87E		13p27	
716	IV–		Nottingham-Cardiff	DMU			13.35	13.43	
717	IV05		Relief Portsmouth-Cardiff	5971	*Merevale Hall*	81A	13.36	13.38	
718	IV07		Portsmouth-Cardiff	D7083		86A	13.40	13.45	
304	IF30	10.25	Paignton-Carmarthen	D1739		?	13.56	14.00	
719	6V21		Freight	D1596		?	14.09		Also seen at Gloucester
720	IF31	08.00	Paddington-Swansea	D7030		86A		14p11	
306	IM95		Newquay-Manchester	D1590		?		14p20	

TABLE THIRTEEN (continued)

Train Ref. No.	Rep. No.	Time	Description	Motive power	Name	Allocation	Time		Remarks
							Arr.	Dep.	
307	IM93	10.45	Kingswear-Liverpool	D1736		86A		14p32	From Gloucester Line
721			Freight	2231		86E	14.35		
722			Portsmouth-Cardiff	D7000		82A	14.59	15.01	
723		13.55	Weston-super-Mare-Cardiff	DMU			15.16	15.20	
309	IT33	12.05	Minehead & Ilfracombe-Cardiff	D1073	*Western Bulwark*	81A	15p24		
724	IE20		Newcastle-Cardiff	D1022	*Western Sentinel*	86A	15p26		Locomotives changed at Gloucester
318	IT35	12.10	Paignton-Cardiff	D7036		86A	15p56		
725	IV11		Portsmouth-Cardiff	D7087		86A	16.02	16.06	
726	IF44		-Swansea	D1587		87F	16.18	16.21	Possibly Ex Paddington
727	IV44		Newcastle-Cardiff	73024			16.23	16.34	
728	IF45		Paddington-Swansea	D1692		82A	16.33	16.38	Locomotives changed at Gloucester
729 [3]			Chepstow-Severn Tunnel Junction-Preston	DMU			16.42		
325	IM92		Paddington-Swansea	44777		2E	16p46		
730	IF46		Penzance-Manchester	D1748			17p04		
329	IM96	10.50	Gloucester-Cardiff	D1594			17p13		
731	2T62		Bristol Stapleton Road-Cardiff	DMU			17.21	17.25	
732			Pilning-Severn Tunnel Junc. Car Carrier	DMU			17p21		
733			Freight	4137		86E	17.31		
734			Bristol-Cardiff	48680		2F	17.44		Also noted at Gloucester
735	2T02	11.20	Penzance-Swansea	D70XX			17.55	17.56	Locomotive not identified
336	IF59		Paddington-Swansea	D1720		82A	18p03		
736	IF54		Chepstow-Cardiff	D1718		86A	18p08		
737			Freight	DMU			18.16	18.18	
738			Leeds-Cardiff	3838		86E	18.31		From Gloucester route
739	IV62		Paddington-Fishguard Harbour	D7046		82A	18p35		Locomotives changed at Gloucester
740	IF60		Parcels	D1055	*Western Advocate*	87E	18p40		
741	3T10		Bristol-Cardiff	D7034		86A	18p46		From Gloucester Route
742	2T02		Paddington-Fishguard Harbour	D1742		86A	18.59	19.03	
743	IF58		Paddington-Fishguard Harbour	D1058	*Western Nobleman*	87E	19p15		

68

TABLE THIRTEEN (continued)

Train Ref. No.	Rep. No.	Time	Description	Motive power	Name	Allocation	Time Arr.	Dep.	Remarks
744	IT43		Portsmouth-Cardiff	D7012		82A		19p25	
745			Chepstow-Severn Tunnel Junction	DMU			19.32		

SEVERN TUNNEL JUNCTION: An empty car train for Severn Tunnel Junction leaves Pilning on 16th May 1964 hauled by 2-6-2T 4150.

(Rodney Lissenden)

TABLE FOURTEEN

SURVEY POINT: SEVERN TUNNEL JUNCTION – EASTBOUND – 25th JULY 1964

Train Ref. No.	Rep. No.	Time	Description	Motive power	Name	Allocation	Arr.	Dep.	Remarks
746		07.05	Swansea-Weston-super-Mare	DMU			09.34	09.36	
747	2.01		Cardiff-Portsmouth	D1742		86A	09.44	09.45	
748	IM28		Cardiff-Newcastle	D1022	Western Sentinel	86A		09p49	
749	IA24		Swansea-Paddington	D1023	Western Fusilier	86A	10.08	10.10	
750			Relief Cardiff-Bournemouth	5979	Cruckton Hall	85B	10.17	10.18	
751	2B		Cardiff-Cheltenham	DMU			10.28	10.29	
752	1057		Cardiff-Bournemouth	D7085		86A	10p37		
753	IA29		Relief to Paddington	D1718		86A	10p49		Origin not established
374	IC58	07.50	Llanelli-Minehead & Ilfracombe	D1739			10p53		
754	IA28		Swansea-Paddington	D1748			11p00		
755			Freight	7318		86G	11p04		Also seen at Gloucester
756	1058		Cardiff-Portsmouth	D7042		82A	11.16	11.18	
375	IC53	10.45	Cardiff-Kingswear	D1736		86A	11p23		
377	IC63		Relief-Paignton	D1752			11p32		Origin not established
380	IC64	08.00	Carmarthen-Penzance	D7001		82A	11p53		
757	IA45		Swansea-Paddington	D1584			12p02		
758	IA38		Relief-Paddington	D1055	Western Advocate	87E	12p04		Origin not established
759			Llanelli-Brockenhurst	6810	Blakemere Grange	87A	12.14	12.16	
760	A2		Newport-Chepstow	DMU			12.24	12.27	
761	IC76		Carmarthen-Taunton	D1073	Western Bulwark	81A	12.40	12.43	Arrival not recorded at Taunton. D7038 (86A) replaced D1073 at Bristol
762	IM76		Pembroke Dock-Derby	D7034		86A		12p43	
763	2C7		Cardiff-Cheltenham	DMU			12.52	12.55	
385		12.20	Cardiff-Newton Abbot	DMU				12p55	
388	IV88	08.20	Manchester-Penzance	D1712		2B	13p03		
764	1061		Cardiff-Portsmouth Harbour	D7094		86A	13.30	13.32	
389	IV89	08.45	Liverpool-Kingswear	D1583			13p36		
392	IV92	09.05	Manchester-Paignton	D1720		82A	13p43		
393	IV93	09.20	Liverpool-Plymouth	D1594			13p49		
765			Freight	6876	Kingsland Grange	86E	13p57		Tunnel route

TABLE FOURTEEN (continued)

Train Ref. No.	Rep. No.	Time	Description	Motive power	Name	Allocation	Time Arr.	Time Dep.	Remarks
766	1A56		Pembroke Dock-Paddington	D1047	Western Lord	86A		14p10	
767	A2		Newport-Chepstow	DMU			14.13	14.14	
768			Freight	3859		86E		14p38	Tunnel Route. Assisted by 4137 (86E)
769			Severn Tunnel Junc.-Pilning Car Carrier	4144		86E		14.41	
770			Cardiff-Cheltenham	DMU			14.41	14.44	
771				45061		12A		14p53	Tunnel route. Assisted by 4121 (86E), train not identified
772	1N61		Cardiff-Leeds	D7019		82A	15.02		Locomotives changed at Gloucester
773	2		Cardiff-Severn Tunnel Junc.	DMU					
774	1A		Cardiff-Bristol	DMU			15.10	15.14	
775	5E76		Freight	D1603		86A		15p24	Gloucester route
776	3A24		Parcels	D7091		86A		15p54	Gloucester route
777			Pembroke Dock-Paddington	D1036	Western Emperor	86A		16p04	
778			Swansea-Bristol	DMU			16.11	16.13	
779			Freight	3844		86G		16p19	
780	6A90		Freight	D1046	Western Marquis	86A		16p28	Tunnel Route. Assisted by 4115 (86E)
781			Freight	44811		15A		16p33	Tunnel route
782	1A80		Cardiff-Cheltenham	DMU			16.39	16.40	Gloucester route
783			Swansea-Paddington	D1014	Western Leviathen	86A		17p00	Gloucester route
784			Freight	6863	Dolhywel Grange	88A		17p03	
785	3H10		Cardiff-Portsmouth	D7066		86A	17.12	17.14	
404	1V95	12.25	Manchester-Plymouth	D1691		86A	17.17	17.21	
786	A2		Newport-Chepstow	DMU			17.23	17.25	
787	1M78		Cardiff-Derby	DMU				17p46	
788			Severn Tunnel Junction-Chepstow	DMU				17.58	
789	C.7		Swansea-Bristol	DMU			18.07	18.12	
790			Freight	3810		87A		18p16	Tunnel Route . Assisted by 4144 (86E)
791	2H86		Severn Tunnel Junction-Pilning Car Carrier	D7083		86A		18p23	Train not identified-Gloucester route.
792				4137		86E		18.46	
793			Freight	6847	Tidmarsh Grange	88A		18p55	
794	1A96		Swansea-Paddington	D1045	Western Viscount	86A	18.59	19.03	Tunnel route

TABLE FOURTEEN (continued)

Train Ref. No.	Rep. No.	Time	Description	Motive power	Name	Allocation	Time Arr.	Time Dep.	Remarks
795			Freight	3818		86G		19p11	Gloucester route
796	2C7		Cardiff-Cheltenham	DMU				19p20	
797	IA97		Swansea-Paddington	D1058	*Western Nobleman*	87E		19p30	
798			Freight	6864	*Dymock Grange*	2B		19p35	Gloucester route
799			Freight	7226		86E		19p40	Tunnel route

TABLE FIFTEEN

SURVEY POINT: SEVERN TUNNEL JUNCTION – WESTBOUND – 21ST AUGUST 1965

Train Ref. No.	Rep. No.	Time	Description	Motive power	Name	Allocation	Arr.	Dep.	Remarks
800	IC97	06.45	Taunton-Swansea	D1657		87E	09.18	09.20	
801	IM84	08.50	Bristol-Liverpool	D1674	Samson	86A		09p25	
802	IV00	07.32	Salisbury-Cardiff	DMU				09p35	
803	2T02	08.30	Cheltenham-Cardiff	D7035		86A	09.37	09.40	
804	IV69	07.10	Derby-Pembroke Dock	D1602		86A		09p54	
805	IF11	08.00	Paddington-Fishguard Harbour	D7023		82A		10p08	
				D1064	Western Regent	87E			
806	2T02	09.10	Weston-Super-Mare-Swansea	D7041		82A		10p16	
807	J87		Pilning-Severn Tunnel Junc. Car Carrier	D6926		86A	10.20		
808	2A3	08.50	Paddington-Fishguard Harbour	D1667		87E		10p42	
809	IF15	09.00	Paddington-Swansea	D1018	Western Buccaneer	87E		10p55	
810		08.22	Weymouth Town-Cardiff	DMU			11.11	11.15	
405	IF18	07.00	Plymouth-Swansea	D7050		82A		11p40	
811			Freight	92129		2D		11p41	Tunnel Route
812	7F04		Freight	D1070	Western Gauntlet	87E	11.55		
410	IM87	08.30	Paignton-Manchester	D1777		41A		12p05	
813	2T02	11.15	Gloucester-Cardiff	D7084		86A	12.05	12.08	
814	IF20	10.00	Paddington-Pembroke Dock	D7033		86A		12p15	
418	IM89	09.12	Paignton-Manchester	D1744		86A		12p23	
815	IV06	09.28	Portsmouth Harbour-Cardiff	D1722		87E		12p32	
412	IM90	09.18	Exmouth & Ilfracombe-Manchester	D1755		86A		12p41	
816	IF27	11.00	Paddington-Swansea	D1586		87E		12p52	
421	IM91	06.30	Penzance-Manchester	D1615		86A		13p01	
817	IV78	07.25	York-Cardiff	D1599		82A		13p07	
818			Train not identified	DMU			13.22	13.23	Tunnel route
819	1024	10.29	Portsmouth Harbour-Cardiff	D1738		82A		13p32	
820	B		Train not identified	DMU				13p53	Tunnel route
426	IF30	10.25	Paignton-Carmarthen	D1691		86A		14p02	

Train Ref. No.	Rep. No.	Time	Description	Motive power	Name	Allocation	Time Arr.	Time Dep.	Remarks
429	IM95	08.00	Newquay-Manchester	D1736		82A		14p18	
430	IM93	10.45	Kingswear-Manchester	D1645		87E		14p27	
821			Freight	4671		86E		14p45	From Gloucester route
822	8B07		Train consisted of withdrawn locos. 4110/44/56/7						
823		13.55	Weston-super-Mare-Cardiff	D6972		86A		14p50	Tunnel route
433	2C33	10.20	Ilfracombe & Minehead-Cardiff	DMU				15p13	
824	2T02	14.30	Gloucester-Cardiff	D7029		86A		15p25	
825		12.03	Portsmouth Harbour-Cardiff	D7038		84A	15.25	15.28	
826	7-31		Freight	D1721		82A		15p44	Also seen at Gloucester
441	IM96	08.55	Penzance-Manchester	D1656		87E		15p52	
827	IV1	15.15	Cheltenham-Cardiff	D42		82A		15p56	
828	IV30	13.08	Portsmouth & Southsea-Cardiff	D7044		82A		16p01	
829	IF45	14.00	Paddington-Swansea	D1666	Odin	82A		16p11	
450	IT35	13.50	Paignton-Cardiff	D1662	Isambard Kingdom Brunel	87E	16.20	16.22	
830	3T57		E.C.S.	DMU		87E		16p44	Tunnel route
831	IF46	15.00	Paddington-Swansea	D7031		86A		16p51	
832	2T02	16.10	Cheltenham-Cardiff	D7084		86A	17.17	17p03 17.19	
833	2T02	17.00	Bristol-Cardiff	D1729		82A	17.35	17.38	
834			Freight	5235		86B		17p43	Also seen at Gloucester
456	IF59	11.30	Penzance-Swansea	D1659		87E		17p52	
835	IF54	16.00	Paddington-Swansea	D1661	North Star	87E		18p10	

TABLE SIXTEEN

SURVEY POINT: SEVERN TUNNEL JUNCTION – EASTBOUND – 21st AUGUST 1965

P = Passing time

Train Ref. No.	Rep. No.	Time	Description	Motive power	Name	Allocation	Time Arr.	Time Dep.	Remarks
836		09.20	Severn Tunnel Junc.-Pilning Car Carrier	D6955		86A		09.24	
837	B2	08.50	Cardiff-Cheltenham	DMU			09.29	09.30	
838	B0	07.35	Swansea-Weston-super-Mare	DMU			09.34	09.35	
839	1A24	08.20	Swansea-Paddington	D1663	*Sir Daniel Gooch*	87E		10p03	
840	2B31	09.42	Cardiff-Gloucester	D7084		86A	10.11	10.12	
841	3X13		E.C.S.	44900		12A		10p27	Tunnel route
490	1C58	08.10	Llanelli-Penzance	D1658		87E		10p44	
842	1A2.	10.15	Cardiff-Paddington	D7031		86A		10p50	
843			Freight	92203		2D		10p59	Also noted at Gloucester
844	1A82	09.20	Swansea-Paddington	D1677		86A		10p59	
845		10.38	Cardiff-Portsmouth Harbour	DMU				11p07	
846			Freight	7029	*Clun Castle*	85B		11p21	Also noted at Gloucester
847			Freight	48060		16C		11p29	Gloucester route
494	1C55	08.00	Carmarthen-Paignton	D1691		86A	11.33	11.34	
496	1C59	10.50	Cardiff-Ilfracombe & Minehead	D1645		87E		11p39	
848	Z71	10.20	Swansea-Paddington	D1681		86A		12p04	
849	1O59	09.30	Llanelli-Bournemouth	D1610		86A	12.11	12.25	
499	1V88	08.20	Manchester-Paignton	D1737		82A		12p21	
505	1V89	08.45	Liverpool-Plymouth	{D1698 / D6904}		86A	12.32	12.43	
510	1C78	09.40	Carmarthen-Taunton	D1662	*Isambard Kingdom Brunel*	86A	12.35	12.39	
850	1N89	08.40	Pembroke Dock-Derby	D1602		87E		12p44	
851	1B36	12.20	Cardiff-Gloucester	D7035		86A	12.51	12.54	
852	1A46	09.05	Pembroke Dock-Paddington	D1601		87E		13p01	
507	1V92	09.05	Manchester-Penzance	D6897		87E		13p11	
508	1V93	09.20	Liverpool-Paignton	D1656		87E		13p23	
853	1061	12.38	Cardiff-Portsmouth & Southsea	DMU			13.27	13.29	

TABLE SIXTEEN (continued)

Train Ref. No.	Rep. No.	Time	Description	Motive power	Name	Allocation	Time Arr.	Time Dep.	Remarks
854	6H61		Freight	D7051		82A		13p30	Gloucester route
855	1A56	12.20	Swansea-Paddington	D1055	Western Advocate	87E		14p03	
856		14.20	Freight	92226		86E		14p10	Tunnel route
857			Severn Tunnel Junc.-Pilning Car Carrier	D6955		86A		14.20	
858	2B31	13.50	Cardiff-Cheltenham	D7084		86A	14.30	14.32	
859	1A56		Freight	D1012	Western Firebrand	87E		14p41	Gloucester route
860	1N40	14.20	Cardiff-York	D1599		82A		14p53	
861	·87		Freight	{D6926 / D7041}		86A / 82A		15p03	
862	1063	14.38	Cardiff-Weymouth	DMU			15.11	15.12	via Bristol
863	6E71		Freight	D1756		86A	15.29		Also noted at Gloucester
864	1A72	11.50	Pembroke Dock-Paddington	D1612		82A		16p12	
865		15.38	Cardiff-Bristol	DMU			16.22	16.23	
519	1V95	12.58	Manchester-Plymouth	D1742		86A		16p26	
866	4B05		E.C.S.	D1697		86A		16p36	
867	B2	15.55	Cardiff-Gloucester	DMU			16.40	16.41	To Bristol, arrive 17.12
868			Freight	D6902		86A		16p41	
869	1A80	15.20	Swansea-Paddington	D1064	Western Regent	87E		17p04	Tunnel route
870	1065	16.38	Cardiff-Portsmouth	DMU			17.16	17.19	
871	2B31	16.55	Cardiff-Cheltenham	D7035		86A	17.27	17.29	
872	3A25		Milk Tanks	D1053	Western Patriarch	82A	17.34		
873	1E29	17.20	Cardiff-Sheffield	D42		82A		17p56	
874			Freight	44714		5D		18p02	
875	1A90	16.20	Swansea-Paddington	D1066	Western Prefect	87E		18p06	Gloucester route
876	J02	17.38	Cardiff-Plymouth	D6936		86A	18.11	18.13	

6. Gloucester – 1962-1965

The observer at Gloucester was located at Barnwood Junction. The 1960s layout at Gloucester was different to that of today with Eastgate station being served by Midland Line trains. Western services to Cheltenham plus all the Midland Line trains could be observed at this location but not the Western trains going East via Stroud to Swindon. The Gloucester observer was also somewhat late in getting started and so many Southbound holiday trains had already passed the location by the time he arrived. Nonetheless the observations are of great interest, particularly in the range of depots supplying motive power. Although this book is primarily concerned with Western Region motive power changes the LM line at Gloucester is worthy of inclusion both because

some of the Peaks and Brush Type 4s used were shedded at Bristol Bath Road and because in subsequent years the locomotives worked right through to the trains' destination. Also recorded were the last year's services via the Somerset and Dorset to the South coast.

1962 – Southbound Bristol/Bath line services
Peaks had already made an impact on services on this line in 1962 with the first trains noted, Nottingham-Plymouth and Sheffield-Paignton being so worked.

The third train was via the Western route (Wolverhampton-Kingswear) and was Castle hauled followed by an unidentified service which ran through to the South West and was hauled by a Doncaster B1. Following this was

GLOUCESTER: The 94XX series pannier tanks were regular performers on Cheltenham-Paddington expresses for the leg from/to Gloucester from where larger motive power worked to Paddington. 9471 is seen on a typical early 1960s working at Cheltenham Spa terminus. *(John L. Champion)*

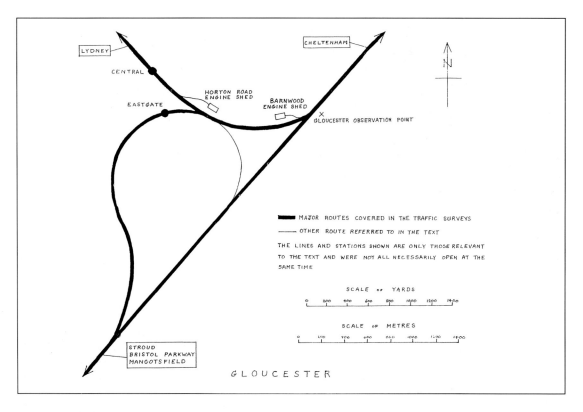

GLOUCESTER

the 09.22 Derby-Gloucester with a Jubilee. York and Bradford services to Bristol produced two more Peaks before another Western train (Wolverhampton-Minehead/Ilfracombe) came through with a Hall in charge. Quite how a Hurlford Stanier Cl.5 got on the front of a Cleethorpes-Exmouth (via the Somerset & Dorset) remains a mystery. Another Stanier Cl.5 was on Bradford-Bournemouth (again via the S&D).

Newcastle-Paignton had a Jubilee with a Peak on the Sunderland-Bristol service. Two further S&D services (both Manchester-Bournemouth) had a Standard Cl.5 and a Peak respectively as motive power, with a Stanier Cl.5 on a third portion of this train. Another Standard version of the type worked a Bradford-Paignton. A straying Templecombe Standard Cl.4 had charge of a Worcester-Bristol local. York and Newcastle to Bristol services were Peak worked.

Gloucester trains that got through to Bristol before observations started at the former were *097* (unidentified) headed by 45088, a Walsall-Kingswear with a Jubilee, Birmingham-Penzance (Castle), Derby-Weston-super-Mare (Peak) and Leicester-Paignton (Stanier Cl.5).

1962 Northbound
Early services were Weston-super-Mare-Sheffield *(1051)* – a Stanier Cl.5 and Paignton-Bradford *(1052)* – Jubilee with a Peak on Bristol-Newcastle *(878)*.

Observations at Gloucester produced train *882,* a York service ex-Cardiff, then ex-S&D Bournemouth-Derby (Jubilee), Bournemouth-Liverpool (Peak), Bournemouth-Manchester (Standard Cl.5) and an unidentified train *888* (Stanier Cl.5).

Meanwhile Paignton-Newcastle came up with a Jubilee as did Paignton-Derby but Paignton-Nottingham was a Stanier Cl.5 although Paignton-Leeds rated a double headed Jubilee and Stanier Cl.5.

The Kingswear and Newton Abbot trains to Bradford were both handled by Peaks, Kingswear-Wolverhampton by a Castle, Newquay-Newcastle by a Jubilee and Paignton-Nottingham *(032)* by a Peak. 14.15 Bristol-York was also Peak worked but Weston-super-Mare-

GLOUCESTER: Even in 1961, Peaks allocated to Bath Road, had made their mark on some services on the Birmingham line as can be seen from the view of D37 on 12.37 Newcastle-Bristol near Ashchurch. Note the Gresley coach, no doubt added to strengthen the weekday formation. By 1962 the train had been slightly refined to 12.40 and was a duty for a Derby-based loco (train *940*). 29th July 1961.   *(Michael Mensing)*

GLOUCESTER: Jubilee 45562 *Alberta* departs from Bath Green Park with a Bournemouth-Bradford service in the last year of through S&D services. Our observation team would see this service only at Gloucester. 4th August 1962.   *(Hugh Ballantyne)*

GLOUCESTER: Still carrying its Southbound reporting number, 7026 *Tenby Castle* is captured near Coaley South with the 14.08 Weston-Wolverhampton on 7th July 1962. Three weeks later, on survey day, the train was in the hands of 7012 *Barry Castle* (see train *903*). *(Michael Mensing)*

Wolverhampton had a Castle (train *903*).

An ex-S&D service to Manchester (train *894*) was headed by a Stanier Cl.5 before the ultimate rarity – a Perth Standard Cl.5 on train *897* to Sheffield. A final S&D train was Exmouth-Cleethorpes with a Stanier Cl.5. The Minehead/Ilfracombe - Wolverhampton with a Penzance County (see Page 22) was a through working followed by a Stanier Cl.5 on Penzance-Bradford. Paignton-Wolverhampton (Castle), Newquay-Wolverhampton (Hall) and Newquay-York (Peak) were next. A final Paignton-Wolverhampton service (Hall) did not reach Gloucester before the survey finished.

1963 Northbound
Services originating South of Taunton produced few changes in the types of motive power employed. Strangers noted were 45102

(Blackpool) to Derby (train *156*) and 73158 (Bedford) bound for Bradford (train *191*). A Mexborough B1 was employed on train *1128* Paignton-Bradford (only recorded at Bristol), similar power taking the Weston-super-Mare-Sheffield throughout with a third example on train *948,* Bristol-Sheffield. The number of Jubilees showed a marked decrease. It must be noted however that all the former S&D services had by now been re-routed away from this line.

1963 Southbound
Strangers in evidence were 45197 from Cricklewood (Bradford-Paignton) and 45246 of Newton Heath on the Newcastle-Paignton.

1964
There was a reduction in the amount of

GLOUCESTER: The last year of through S&D services was 1962 and IM09 12-20 Bournemouth West-Nottingham is in the hands of Stanier Class 5 44658. Train *904* with reporting number IM00 was probably the same service in the survey taken on 28th July 1962. West of Coaley Station, 7th July 1962.

(Michael Mensing)

Northbound steam activity but the only diesel power remained the Peaks. Steam strangers continued to appear on the Midland line with B1s again performing along with a Newton Heath Jubilee and a Willesden Stanier Cl.5.

Power for the Western Region services to the West Midlands continued exclusively steam.

Southbound – a similar "squeeze" on steam power was observed.

1965

In the space of a year Northbound steam had been ousted from its Midland main line role, its place having been taken by Brush Type 4s, with Bath Road, Landore and Tinsley examples being the main performers, with D1874 being the highest noted. Steam power hung on to a few Western diagrams with train *427* to Wolverhampton, and train *451* also to Wolverhampton providing work for Halls.

Southbound – Stanier Cl.5s managed to work diagrams via the WR route on two trains but again for all LMR routed trains diesel power in the form of Peaks or Brush Type 4s was provided.

These Wolverhampton-Bristol runs were thus the only main line steam passenger duties

GLOUCESTER: Steam still had a role to play at Gloucester in 1964. 2-6-2 tank 4107 stands in the foreground of this view taken at the South end of Gloucester Central Station. It had probably just arrived with a Cheltenham-Paddington working which would reverse here going forward behind a Hymek. Arriving from the South is Hymek D7033 on the afternoon Cardiff-Leeds working which four weeks earlier had been worked by D7019 (see train *772*). A Peak would be the likely motive power beyond Gloucester for this train. (22nd August 1964)   *(R. E. Toop)*

recorded in the survey of 1965. They were also unusual on this date in that at this time Oxley had some Britannia Pacifics allocated which were used on these diagrams on most Saturdays in 1965.

Local traffic at Gloucester
This amounted only to stopping trains to Birmingham, the Gloucester-Cheltenham workings of the expresses from Paddington, some freight workings not seen elsewhere plus light engine movements to the depots.

Gloucester-Cheltenham trains were worked by a variety of "local" power. 1962 saw Pannier

8491, 2251 class 3202 and 2-6-2 tank 6137 so employed. Freight traffic saw appearances by 0-6-0 44165 and WD 90218 whilst light engines included dock tank 41535, Pannier 6424 and various diesel shunters. Ivatt 43046 brought in a Worcester-Gloucester local.

1963 Gloucester-Cheltenham services utilised 4109, 7335, 5184, 4100, 4109 and 4614 but the Birmingham local service was DMU worked. LMS 0-6-0s continued their presence plus a Cl.9F on a freight. 78006/9 allocated to Gloucester Barnwood enlivened the light engine scene.

1964

Gloucester-Birmingham locals were operated by a Standard and Stanier Cl.5s, the Cheltenham portion of the Paddington trains by 5184, 8409, 9606/8 and 9471 and several freights by Cl.9Fs (including an ex-Crosti boilered variety and 92220 *Evening Star*). A former LMS 0-6-0 was still to be seen with a newcomer to the light engine scene, D2137.

1965

Super power had come to the Paddington line services, these being in the hands of Westerns and Hymeks. The local service to Birmingham had ceased and freight traffic was shared between steam and diesel traction. With the demise of Barnwood shed light engine activity was greatly reduced but one constant remained – an LMS 0-6-0.

NB – the light engine movements have not been included in the survey Gloucester tables unless they were 'through workings'.

GLOUCESTER: Almost any locomotive could appear on the Birmingham-Bristol "stoppers". The service did not survive to have a direct replacement by diesel traction. Standard Class 5 73096 stands at the now demolished Gloucester Eastgate station with the 18.30 Bristol-Birmingham New Street service on 7th July 1962. *(Michael Mensing)*

GLOUCESTER: The change-over. The scene was repeated across the Western Region – Castle 5017 *The Gloucestershire Regiment 28th, 61st* on the 13.45 Paddington-Cheltenham passes D7001 which was in charge of 14.00 Cheltenham-Swindon slow. Kemble. 24th February 1962.   *(B. W. L. Brooksbank)*

GLOUCESTER: Service IN40 was the 10.20 Newton Abbot-Bradford in 1964. On the survey date it was entrusted to 45674 from Saltley depot (train *301*). One week later the observers at Wickwar could record only a Stanier Cl.5 44825 on this turn.   *(Peter W. Gray)*

TABLE SEVENTEEN

SURVEY POINT: GLOUCESTER – NORTHBOUND – 28th JULY 1962

Train Ref. No.	Rep. No.	Time	Description	Motive power	Name	Allocation	Arr.	Dep.	Remarks
877		09.26	Cardiff-Cheltenham	DMU				11p20	
878	IN70	10.20	Bristol-Newcastle	D42		82A		11p23	
879			Train not identified	6394		85B		11p42	
880		11.46	Gloucester-Cheltenham	8491		85B		11p51	
881			Freight	44165		21A		11p57	
882	IN14	10.15	Cardiff-York	73094		85C		12p02	
883	IH55	11.45	Cheltenham-Paddington	Castle				12p13	
884			Paddington-Cheltenham	6137		85B		12p17	
002	IN61	07.45	Paignton-Newcastle-on-Tyne	45656	Cochrane	41A		12p57	
010	IN67	09.00	Paignton-Leeds	{ 45088 / 45685	Barfleur }	21A / 82E		13p02	
007	IM18	08.20	Paignton-Nottingham	45272		21A		13p05	
885	IM65	08.40	Bournemouth-Derby	45611	Hong Kong	16A		13p09	
886		13.07	Gloucester-Cheltenham	8491		85B		13p11	
887			Freight	90218		2F		13p15	
888	IM66		Train not identified	45342		17A		13p19	
889	IM02	09.25	Bournemouth-Liverpool	D137		17A		13p29	
890	IM04	09.45	Bournemouth-Manchester	73068		82E		13p30	
018	IN37	09.00	Kingswear-Bradford	D39		82A		13p42	
891	IH16	08.30	Pembroke Dock-Birmingham Snow Hill	4952	Peplow Hall	88A		13p52	
892	IE68	12.15	Weston-super-Mare-Sheffield	44814		21A		14p09	
893		12.15	Cardiff-Cheltenham	DMU				14p18	
894	IM07	10.32	Bournemouth-Manchester	45370		8C		14p25	
021	IN40	10.19	Newton Abbot-Bradford	D88		17A		14p33	
895	2M73	14.31	Gloucester-Birmingham N. St.	D50		17A		14p36	
896		11.35	Paddington-Cheltenham	4101		85B		14p39	
024	IH22	10.05	Kingswear-Wolverhampton	5089	Westminster Abbey	84A		14p46	
897	IE58	11.12	Bournemouth-Sheffield	73005		63A		14p56	
030	IN86	08.43	Newquay-Newcastle	45682	Trafalgar	82E		15p09	
898		12.00	Swansea-Cheltenham	DMU				15p18	

P = Passing time

85

TABLE SEVENTEEN (continued)

Train Ref. No.	Rep. No.	Time	Description	Motive power	Name	Allocation	Arr.	Dep.	Remarks
899	IV67	14.15	Bristol-York	D118		17A		15p21	
900	IE59	10.42	Exmouth-Cleethorpes	44658		16A		15p38	
901			Freight	48361		18A		15p40	
032	IN26	11.35	Paignton-Nottingham	D64		17A		15p47	
902		11.45	Carmarthen-Birmingham	DMU				15p52	
903	IB06	14.08	Weston-super-Mare-Wolverhampton	7012	Barry Castle	84A		15p55	
904	IM00			45221		21A		15p59	Train not identified, Probably ex S&D
905	1081			44806		21A		16p12	Train not identified, Probably ex S&D
906		16.11	Gloucester-Worcester	43046		21A		16p18	
907		16.00	Cheltenham-Paddington	Castle				16p23	Using far side of triangle
908		16.30	Gloucester-Cheltenham	4116		85B		16p35	
038		12.45	Minehead & Ilfracombe-Wolverhampton	1006	County of Cornwall	83G		16p35	
043	IN68	09.05	Penzance-Bradford	45006		21A		16p55	
909		13.45	Paddington-Cheltenham	6137		85B		16p57	
050	IH31	12.55	Paignton-Wolverhampton	5025	Chirk Castle	81F		17p19	
910		15.30	Cardiff-Cheltenham	DMU				17p31	
053	IH34	11.20	Newquay-Wolverhampton	4904	Binnegar Hall	82B		17p36	
911		17.52	Gloucester-Cheltenham	2249		86C		17p59	
056	IN87	11.35	Newquay-York	D16		55H		18p08	

TABLE EIGHTEEN

SURVEY POINT: GLOUCESTER – SOUTHBOUND – 28th JULY 1962

P = Passing time

Train Ref. No.	Rep. No.	Time	Description	Motive power	Name	Allocation	Arr.	Dep.	Remarks
113	IV31	07.43	Nottingham-Plymouth	D64		17A		11p15	
119	IV33	08.00	Sheffield-Paignton	D118		17A		11p29	
912	IA56	11.45	Cheltenham-Paddington	3201		89B		11p58	
124	C79	10.05	Wolverhampton-Kingswear	5025	Chirk Castle	81F		12p15	Train worked beyond Taunton
123	IV34		Not identified	61125		36A		12p16	
913		09.22	Derby-Gloucester	45557	New Brunswick	17A		12p22	
914	IV35	07.20	York-Bristol	D68		14A		12p27	
915	IV36	07.40	Bradford-Bristol	D16		55H		12p41	
916	2T52	12.30	Cheltenham-Cardiff	DMU				12p45	
128	C85	10.55	Wolverhampton-Minehead & Ilfracombe	4906	Bradfield Hall	84B		12p56	
917	092	07.00	Cleethorpes-Exmouth	44992		67B		13p08	
918	2H73	12.20	Worcester-Gloucester	43046		21A		13p22	
919	1094	07.45	Bradford-Bournemouth	44841		21A		13p36	
920	2H81	13.25	Cheltenham-Gloucester	6137		85B		13p39	
134	IV38	07.30	Newcastle-Paignton	45690	Leander	82E		13p56	
135	IV39	09.05	Bradford-Paignton	D128		17A		13p57	
921	2H81	13.50	Cheltenham-Gloucester	4101		85B		14p05	
922	IV40	07.40	Sunderland-Bristol	D95		17A		14p08	
923	1-69		Manchester-Bournemouth	73019		82F		14p36	
924	1095	10.25	Manchester-Bournemouth	D153		17A		14p41	
925	IV70	08.10	Newcastle-Cardiff	D37		82A		14p48	
926		14.45	Cheltenham-Gloucester	6137		85B		14p59	
927	1097	10.55	Manchester-Bournemouth	44963		21A		15p18	
142	IV42	09.20	Bradford-Paignton	73136		17A		15p20	
928		15.25	Cheltenham-Gloucester	DMU				15p40	
929	2B74	14.40	Worcester-Bristol	75002		82G		15p48	
930	IA02	16.00	Cheltenham-Paddington	4116		85B		16p13	
931		16.20	Cheltenham-Gloucester	DMU				16p34	
932			Freight	90524		2F		16p40	
933	IF52	15.45	Birmingham-Swansea	6879	Overton Grange	84E		17p08	

TABLE EIGHTEEN (continued)

Train Ref. No.	Rep. No.	Time	Description	Motive power	Name	Allocation	Time Arr.	Dep.	Remarks
934			Freight	48101		21A		17p10	
935	IV41	10.00	Newcastle-Cardiff	61004	*Oryx*	41A		17p26	
936	IV44	12.52	York-Bristol	D17		55H		17p33	
937		17.32	Cheltenham-Gloucester	6137		85B		17p47	
938		16.50	Worcester-Gloucester	4104		84F		17p53	
939		17.50	Cheltenham-Swindon	4101		85B		18p04	
940	IV45	12.40	Newcastle-Bristol	D91		17A		19p23	

TABLE NINETEEN

SURVEY POINT: GLOUCESTER – NORTHBOUND – 27th JULY 1963

P = Passing time

Train Ref. No.	Rep. No.	Time*	Description	Motive power	Name	Allocation	Arr.	Dep.	Remarks
647		09.26	Cardiff-Birmingham	DMU				11p20	
941			Freight	44123		85C		11p26	
942	IN70	10.20	Bristol-Newcastle	D123		17A		11p34	
943			Gloucester-Birmingham	DMU				11p43	
944			Paddington-Cheltenham	4109		85B		11p56	
945			Freight	92152		21A		11p58	
652	IM31	10.15	Cardiff-Birmingham	73068		85C		12p11	
152	IN61	07.45	Paignton-Newcastle	D104		17A		12p20	
946			Paddington-Cheltenham	7335		85B		12p37	
155	IM18	08.20	Paignton-Nottingham	45260		21A		12p39	
156	IM20		Relief to Derby	45102		24E		12p42	
158	IN48	09.00	Paignton-Sheffield	73015		82E		12p51	
947		13.07	Gloucester-Cheltenham	5184		85B		13p17	
162	IN37	09.00	Paignton-Bradford	D38		82A		13p22	
948	IE69	12.45	Bristol-Sheffield	61138		41F		13p49	
659	IM72	08.30	Pembroke Dock-Derby	73093		85C		13p56	
949	IE68	12.15	Weston-Super-Mare-Locking Road-Sheffield	61075		41F		14p09	61075 Replaced D147 (17A) at Bristol
660		12.15	Cardiff-Cheltenham	DMU				14p18	
169	3B	10.19	Newton Abbot-Bradford	44810		21A		14p26	
950		14.31	Gloucester-Birmingham New Street	DMU				14p35	
170	IH22	10.05	Kingswear-Wolverhampton	6803	Bucklebury Grange	84B		14p40	
951		11.35	Paddington-Cheltenham	4100		85B		14p50	
179	IN86	08.43	Newquay-Newcastle	D110		17A		15p00	
952	IM09		Bournemouth-Nottingham	D147		17A		15p13	
953	IN84	14.15	Bristol-York	45674	Duncan	21A		15p23	
666		12.00	Swansea-Cheltenham	DMU				15p25	
954			Freight	5939	Tangley Hall	86A		15p32	
180	IM23	11.35	Paignton-Nottingham	D111		17A		15p40	
955	IH28	14.08	Weston-super-Mare-Wolverhampton	6842	Nunhold Grange	84F		15p51	

TABLE NINETEEN (continued)

Train Ref. No.	Rep. No.	Time*	Description	Motive power	Name	Allocation	Time Arr.	Time Dep.	Remarks
956			Gloucester-Cheltenham	4109		85B		16p10	
671	1N61		Cardiff-Leeds	45626	*Seychelles*	16D		16p14	
667	4E71		Freight	D1041	*Western Prince*	88A		16p20	
957		16.30	Gloucester-Cheltenham	4614		85C		16p33	
958		13.45	Paddington-Cheltenham	4100		85B		16p53	
191	1N68	09.05	Penzance-Bradford	73158		14E		16p59	
186	2C83	12.45	Minehead & Ilfracombe-Wolverhampton	6904	*Charfield Hall*	84C		17p03	
195	1E70		Paignton-Sheffield	D40		82A		17p22	
677		15.30	Cardiff-Cheltenham	6381		85B		17p33	
199	1H34	11.20	Newquay-Wolverhampton	7024	*Powis Castle*	84A		17p36	
959		17.52	Gloucester-Cheltenham	2286		86B		17p58	
202	1E24		Penzance-Sheffield	D20		55H		18p03	
203	1A87	11.35	Newquay-York	D90		17A		18p14	
688	1M28		Cardiff-Birmingham	DMU				18p37	

* The 1963 Working Timetable was not available. Where the service was identical to that in 1962 the 1962 origin departure time is quoted.

TABLE TWENTY

SURVEY POINT: GLOUCESTER – SOUTHBOUND – 27th JULY 1963

P = Passing time

Train Ref. No.	Rep. No.	Time*	Description	Motive power	Name	Allocation	Arr.	Dep.	Remarks
252	IV31	07.43	Nottingham-Plymouth	45667	*Jellicoe*	17B		11p20	
259	IV34		Sheffield-Paignton	D40		82A		11p35	
960	IV35	07.20	York-Bristol	D93		17A		11p45	
961	IA56	11.45	Cheltenham-Paddington	5184		85B		11p57	
962	IV36	07.40	Bradford-Bristol	D20		55H		12p05	
260	IC79	10.05	Wolverhampton-Kingswear	7024	*Powis Castle*	84A		12p24	
612	IV71		Nottingham-Cardiff	DMU				12p36	
626			Freight	92208		88A		13p38	
963	IV37		Hull-Bristol	D32		55H		13p41	
964	2H81	13.50?	Cheltenham-Gloucester	DMU				13p54	
622	0Z52		Light Engine	D1054	*Western Governor*	88A		14p04	
965			Train not identified	4109		85B		14p23	Origin not identified
620	IV60		-Cardiff	45653	*Barham*	21A		14p29	
273	IV40	09.20	Bradford-Paignton	45197		6G		14p33	
277	IV38	07.30	Newcastle-Paignton	45246		12B		15p03	
623	IV70	08.10	Newcastle-Cardiff	D168		52A		15p08	
278	IV39	09.05	Bradford-Paignton	D30		55H		15p17	
966			Train not identified	44966		21A		15p40	Train possibly terminated at Gloucester (Loco L · E to depot)
631			Cheltenham-Cardiff	DMU				15p42	
967			Newcastle-Bristol	D163	*Leicestershire and Derbyshire Yeomanry*			15p59	
968	IV43		Newcastle-Bristol	D33		17A		16p02	
969		16.00	Cheltenham-Paddington	4109		82A		16p14	
970			Train not identified	DMU		85B		16p35	
971			Train not identified	DMU				17p16	
972			Freight	92107		21A		17p18	
637	IV69		Train not identified	D18		55H		17p38	
973			Birmingham-Gloucester	43122		21A		18p01	
974			Train not identified	4109		85B		18p02	
975			Freight	48463		85C		18p21	
976	IV45		Newcastle-Bristol	D12		55H		18p25	

* The 1963 Working Timetable was not available. Where the service was identical to that in 1962 the 1962 origin departure time is quoted.

P = Passing time

TABLE TWENTY-ONE

SURVEY POINT: GLOUCESTER – NORTHBOUND – 25th JULY 1964

Train Ref. No.	Rep. No.	Time*	Description	Motive power	Name	Allocation	Arr.	Dep.	Remarks
977			Freight	44123		85B		11p23	
978		DMU	Train not identified						
979	IT70		Bristol-Newcastle	D120		16C		11p35	
980			Train not identified	DMU				11p42	
981			Gloucester-Cheltenham	9471		85B		11p48	
982			Freight	44914		2F		11p56	
983			Paddington-Cheltenham	5184		85B		12p19	
284	IN79	07.50	Paignton-Newcastle	61315		41D		12p28	
287	IM18	08.20	Paignton-Nottingham	D93		16C		12p33	
755			Freight	7318		86G		12p48	
291	IN48	09.00	Paignton-Leeds	45602	*British Honduras*	9D		12p58	
296	IN37	09.10	Kingswear-Bradford	D119		16C		13p22	
984	IN20		Weston-super-Mare-Bimingham New Street.	D99		16C		13p32	
985	IE68		Weston-super-Mare-Shefffield	61394		41F		13p44	
986			Paddington-Cheltenham	5184				13p46	
762	IM76		Pembroke Dock-Derby	44965		85B		13p56	
763	2C7		Cardiff-Cheltenham	DMU		2E		14p16	
301	IN40	10.20	Newton Abbot-Bradford	45674	*Duncan*	2E		14p19	
302	IM34	10.10	Kingswear-Wolverhampton	6903	*Belmont Hall*	2B		14p30	
987			Gloucester-Cheltenham	DMU				14p34	
311	IN86	08.45	Newquay-Newcastle	D116		16C		14p59	
988	IM84		Paddington-Cheltenham	8409		85D		15p11	
989	IM06		Bristol-York	44810		2E		15p22	
990			Train not identified	45288		1F		15p38	Ex Bournemouth?
312	IM23	11.35	Paignton-Nottingham	45305		1A		15p42	
772	IN61		Cardiff-Leeds	D33		82A		16p07	
770			Cardiff-Cheltenham	DMU				16p10	
315	IM35		Minehead & Ilfracombe-Wolverhampton	7023	*Penrice Castle*	85A		16p16	

TABLE TWENTY-ONE (continued)

Train Ref. No.	Rep. No.	Time	Description	Motive power	Name	Allocation	Arr.	Dep.	Remarks
991			Gloucester-Birmingham	73091		85B		16p18	
992			Freight	92026		15C		16p20	
993			Paddington-Cheltenham	9608		6C		16p33	
994	X20		E.C.S.-Birmingham	DMU				16p37	
320	IE29	09.05	Penzance-Sheffield	D37		82A		16p41	
995			Train not identified	DMU				17p12	
328	IE70	13.00	Paignton-Sheffield	D157		16C		17p30	
331	IH45	11.20	Newquay-Wolverhampton	5063	*Earl Baldwin*	2B		17p34	
996			Paddington-Cheltenham	8409		85D		17p59	
782			Cardiff-Cheltenham	DMU				18p01	
333	IE24	11.00	Penzance-Sheffield	D22		55A		18p05	
334	IN87	11.45	Newquay-York	D42		82A		18p15	

TABLE TWENTY-TWO

SURVEY POINT: GLOUCESTER – SOUTHBOUND – 25th JULY 1964

P = Passing time

Train Ref. No.	Rep. No.	Time	Description	Motive power	Name	Allocation	Time Arr.	Time Dep.	Remarks
997			Freight	92220		88A		11p03	
378	IV33	08.10	Sheffield-Penzance	D42	*Evening Star*	82A		11p03	
379		07.43	Nottingham-Plymouth	44765		5A		11p18	
998			Freight	44123		85B		11p20	
382	IV42		Relief Sheffield-Paignton	44666		2E		11p25	
999			Freight	43017		2E		11p27	
383	IV34	08.15	Sheffield-Paignton	D157		16C		11p36	
1000			Cheltenham-Gloucester	9606		87D		11p51	
1001	IV36		Bradford-Bristol	D22		55A		11p59	
384	IV54	10.05	Wolverhampton-Paignton	6924	*Grantley Hall*	81D		12p20	
716	IV		Nottingham-Cardiff	DMU				12p41	
719	6V21		Freight	D1596				12p54	
1002			Train not identified	DMU				13p08	
1003			Freight	92132		15B		13p20	
1004	IV37		Rotherham-Bristol	D19		55A		13p37	
394	IV38	07.30	Newcastle-Paignton	D138		16C		13p47	
1005			Cheltenham-Gloucester	DMU				13p49	
734			Freight	48680		2F		14p16	
1006			Cheltenham-Paddington	9471		85B		14p22	
397	IV40	09.05	Bradford-Paignton	45608	*Gibraltar*	55A		14p27	
724	IE20		Newcastle-Cardiff	73024		87F		14p35	
727	IV44		Newcastle-Cardiff	D33		82A		14p43	
1007	IX20		Special	DMU				14p46	Train not identified. Returned E.C.S. at 16.37
401	IV39	10.35	Bradford-Paignton	D14		55A		15p06	
1008	2M73		Birmingham-Gloucester	44658		16D		15p36	
1009	2T52		Cheltenham-Gloucester	DMU				15p38	
1010			Cheltenham-Paddington	8409		85B		16p01	
1011	IV25		Newcastle-Bristol	D35		82A		16p13	
1012			Freight	73051		82F		16p32	
1013			Cheltenham-Gloucester	DMU				16p44	

TABLE TWENTY-TWO (continued)

Train Ref. No.	Rep. No.	Time*	Description	Motive power	Name	Allocation	Time Arr.	Dep.	Remarks
1014			Train not identified	73031		85B		16p59	
739	IV62		Leeds-Cardiff	D161		16C		17p33	
1015			Cheltenham-Gloucester	DMU				17p53	
1016			Birmingham-Gloucester	45263		2E		17p56	
1017	IV45		Newcastle-Bristol	D16		55A		18p02	
1018			Cheltenham-Paddington	9606		87D		18p07	

TABLE TWENTY-THREE

SURVEY POINT: GLOUCESTER – NORTHBOUND – 21st AUGUST 1965

P = Passing time

Train Ref. No.	Rep. No.	Time	Description	Motive power	Name	Allocation	Time Arr.	Dep.	Remarks
1019	1N70	10.30	Bristol-Newcastle	D64	Coldstream Guardsman	ML		11p26	
1020	1B55	09.20	Paddington-Cheltenham	D1063	Western Monitor	87E		11p54	
406	1N79	07.30	Paignton-Newcastle	D98		ML		12p03	
1021	4B47		Freight	D1655		87E		12p11	
409	1M18	08.20	Paignton-Nottingham	D44		ML		12p20	
1022		12.30	Gloucester-Cheltenham	DMU				12p36	
415	1N48	09.00	Paignton-Leeds	D88		ML		12p44	
843			Freight	92203		2D		12p53	
420	1N37	09.10	Paignton-Bradford	D89	Honourable Artillery Company	ML		13p17	
850	1N89	08.40	Pembroke Dock-Derby	D1602		86A		13p26	
846			Freight	7029	Clun Castle	85B		13p36	
1023	1E68	12.10	Weston-super-Mare-Sheffield	D1597		82A		13p44	
425	1N40	10.20	Newton-Abbot-Bradford	D1748		82A		14p07	
1024	1N64	13.20	Bristol-York	D25		55A		14p30	
1025		14.21	Gloucester-Stratford Upon Avon	DMU				14p39	
427	1M34	10.05	Paignton-Wolverhampton	7908	Henshall Hall	2A		14p41	
434	1N86	08.45	Newquay-Newcastle	D59	Royal Warwickshire Fusilier	ML		15p05	
858	2B31	13.50	Cardiff-Cheltenham	D7084		86A		15p20	
435	1M23	11.35	Paignton-Nottingham	D95		ML		15p34	
860	1N40	14.20	Cardiff-York	D1599		82A		15p41	
1026	1M22	12.45	Weymouth-Derby	D117		ML		15p52	via Bristol, brought into Bristol by D1872 (41A)
433	2C33	12.17	Minehead & Ilfracombe-Wolverhampton	D1590		87E		15p59	
1027	2B31	16.10	Gloucester-Cheltenham	D7011		82A		16p12	
443	1N87	09.20	Penzance-York	D14		55A		16p34	Train assisted by D1735 (82A) from Bristol to Gloucester
863	6E71		Freight	D1756		86A		16p39	

TABLE TWENTY-THREE (continued)

Train Ref. No.	Rep. No.	Time*	Description	Motive power	Name	Allocation	Arr.	Dep.	Remarks
448	IE70	13.00	Paignton-Sheffield	D1872		41A		17p12	
1028		17.25	Gloucester-Cheltenham	DMU				17p32	
451	IM54	11.20	Penzance-Wolverhampton	6953	Leighton Hall	81F		17p35	
454	IN21	11.00	Penzance-Bradford	D28		55A		17p51	
455	IN54	11.45	Newquay-York	D1874		41A		18p02	
871	2B31	16.55	Cardiff-Cheltenham	D7035		86A		18p16	
1029	2B51	17.45	Gloucester-Cheltenham	D7015		82A		18p18	
873	IE29	17.20	Cardiff-Sheffield	D42		82A		18p36	
1030		18.32	Gloucester-Cheltenham	DMU				18p37	

TABLE TWENTY-FOUR

SURVEY POINT: GLOUCESTER – SOUTHBOUND – 21st AUGUST 1965

Train Ref. No.	Rep. No.	Time	Description	Motive power	Name	Allocation	Time Arr.	Time Dep.	Remarks
1031		10.55	Cheltenham-Gloucester	DMU				11p05	
497	1V32	07.53	Nottingham-Paignton	D95		ML		11p14	
498	1V33	07.02	Bradford-Penzance	D14		55A		11p32	
502	1X98		Relief from Birmingham	44808		2B		12p02	
501	1V34	08.52	Sheffield-Paignton	D1874		41A		12p07	
503	1V54	10.05	Wolverhampton-Kingswear	D1590		87E		12p14	
1032	V28		Train not identified	D177		52A		12p24	
817	1V78	07.25	York-Cardiff	D1599		82A		12p26	
1033	4V50		Freight	D1647		87E		12p46	
1034		12.55	Cheltenham-Gloucester	DMU				13p05	
511	1V37	07.30	Newcastle-Paignton	D169		52A		13p23	
1035			Freight	6924	*Grantley Hall*	81F		13p46	
826	7.31		Freight	D1721		82A		13p57	
834			Freight	5235		86B		14p07	
1036	1V38	08.15	Newcastle-Bristol	D28		55A		14p25	
515	1V39	10.05	Bradford-Paignton	D37		82A		14p31	
516	1V40	09.00	Bradford-Paignton	D124		ML		14p44	
1037		14.55	Cheltenham-Gloucester	DMU				15p07	
1038	6V23		Freight	D1750		86A		15p14	
827	1V·1	15.15	Cheltenham-Cardiff	D42		82A		15p22	
1039			Freight	6813		85A		15p57	
1040	1A76	16.00	Cheltenham-Paddington	D1063	*Eastbury Grange*	87E		16p09	
832	2T02	16.10	Cheltenham-Cardiff	D7084	*Western Monitor*	86A		16p21	
1041	1V43	10.28	Newcastle-Bristol	D35		82A		16p51	
1042			Leamington Spa-Gloucester	DMU				17p02	
1043	7V25		Freight	D1588		87E		17p10	
1044	7V20		Freight	D1587		87E		17p33	
1045	1V45	12.15	Newcastle-Bristol	D21		55A		17p41	
1046	2B29	17.25	Cheltenham-Gloucester	D7011		82A		17p43	
1047		17.55	Cheltenham-Gloucester	DMU				18p05	
1048	1V72	13.45	York-Cardiff	D1739		82A		18p25	

BRISTOL: 6810 *Blakemere Grange* at Lawrence Hill, heads North from Bristol with the 12.00 Kingswear-Manchester on 11th August 1962. There would be plenty of heavy work for the engine with the climb up through Filton, out of the Severn Tunnel and on up over the North and West route. Two weeks earlier the train had been entrusted to a County (train *046*). The coaching stock appears to all be of LMS origin.

(*B. W. L. Brooksbank*)

BRISTOL: A typical scene at Bristol in the Summer of 1963 with the Exmouth-Manchester service headed by the customary Hymek, in this case D7075, having just arrived. This would give way to steam haulage for its journey over the North and West route. Meanwhile Standard Class 5 73167 waits departure on what appears to be an incorrectly head-coded 12.15 Weston-super-Mare (Locking Road)-Sheffield. This train produced a variety of motive power including B1s (see train *940*). 22nd June 1963. (*J. H. Sparkes*)

BRISTOL: An evocative view of the Brunel train shed at Temple Meads with Standard Cl.4 75001 awaiting its next duty. In the rear is a three car Pressed Steel suburban dmu. 23rd April 1963. *(Terry Nicholls)*

BRISTOL: Sunday morning steam shed nostalgia at Barrow Road on 18th October 1964. The volume of apparently active steam at this late date is somewhat deceptive as numbers had been swelled by not only the influx of GW classes following closure of St Philip's Marsh shed but also by one road occupied by condemned engines en route for scrap. *(Terry Nicholls)*

7. Bristol – 1962-1965

Having looked at the traffic at the edges of the area and taken out all the through trains there remains the activity at Bristol to be analysed.

Routes not covered by the foregoing were the Weston-super-Mare-(Bristol)-Paddington services, Bristol-Weymouth, Bristol-Bath Green Park (for the S&D), and local services such as the Severn Beach branch and other stopping services. There were also a large number of light engine and empty coaching stock (ECS) movements in the station area including locomotives coming down from Barrow Road depot, but then reversing round to St. Philip's Marsh to take over trains there to avoid them working through Temple Meads station.

Due to space considerations light engine movements and all through trains recorded at other survey points have been omitted from the data at the end of this chapter.

1962 Northbound

The day started with the departure of a Weymouth service in the hands of a Hall. Various unidentified DMU movements took place before the departure of train *1054* Weston-Paddington with a Hymek in charge. Bristol-Portsmouth and *1059* Weston-Paddington were provided with Halls. All Severn Beach line trains were DMU worked and had been for several years. Conversely the

BRISTOL: New arrival on the Western. Hymek D7000 departing from Bath with the 08.10 Bristol-Portsmouth service complete with Southern Region green stock. Yellow warning panels had yet to appear on the ends of the locomotives. The Hymeks arrived too late in 1961 to make an impression on the level of steam duties on Summer Saturdays but – as can be seen from our surveys – by 1962 they were working much of the Paddington-South Wales service and a large number of the seasonal services to the South-West. 15th July 1961.

(Hugh Ballantyne)

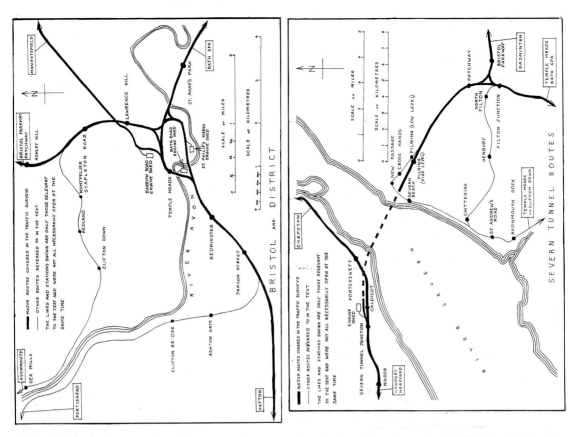

BRISTOL: Train *1094* leaves Bath Spa headed by 6000 *King George V*. Few realised that within a few months this scene would be unrepeatable. The standard train formation is strengthened with at least four coaches of LMS origin. 1963 saw a Hymek on this working, 1964 a Warship and 1965 a Brush Type 4 showing almost perfectly the evolution of Western Region motive power in the period under review. 8.45am Paddington-Weston-super-Mare. 29th July 1962.

(Hugh Ballantyne)

BRISTOL: The scene at Platform Nine at Bristol Temple Meads as 1011 *County of Chester* couples up to work the 09.18 Exmouth-Manchester forward. Behind the engine the pointed roof of the Brunel train shed can be seen where terminating trains from the Midlands could be found as well as seeing use for several of the Severn Beach workings. This view was taken on 10th August 1963. On the survey date in 1963 (27th July) the train was in the hands of Hall 6915 (train *159*). *(D. W. L. Brooksbank)*

BRISTOL: A strange Saturday through working was the 13.12 Calne-Weston-super-Mare seen here at Oldfield Park near Bath with 82035 in charge on the date of the survey in 1963 (train *1180*). In 1964 the train was still steam worked but started at Bristol (train *1245*) and in 1965 became Swindon-Weston with a Hymek in charge (train *1306*). 27th July 1963. *(Hugh Ballantyne)*

BRISTOL: A rarity was the pairing of different diesel classes except over the Devon banks. This 1966 view shows the maroon livery applied to the Warships following initial application to the Westerns. Shortly afterwards came the decision to change to blue as the standard colour and the introduction of full yellow ends. Warship D828 *Magnificent* and Western D1041 *Western Prince* head the 13.45 Paddington - Weston-super-Mare during the first "steamless" season at Bristol. July 1966. *(J. H. Sparkes)*

Bath Green Park service was – with a few exceptions – always in the hands of a 412XX or 82XXX tank.

The local service to Bath Spa was also DMU worked. Following the departure of two Sheffield services (both provided with Jubilees), the Bristol-Paddington service was worked by a Hall, this being preceded by a homebound Weymouth Standard Cl.5. Another Standard Cl.5 worked what was probably a Bath Green Park train but the activities of a 42XX tank and four coaches remain unexplained as does the appearance shortly after of a second member of the class.

The appearance of *King George V* on Weston-Paddington no doubt produced both pride in the older observer and cries of "scrap it" from the youngsters – little realising that this would indeed be the last Summer of the Kings. A DMU headed for Weymouth and there

followed several unidentified Hymek workings interspersed by similar activities with 6986 *Rydal Hall*, 4660, 43963 and 82007. A Weston-Paddington service arrived with a Hymek in charge and exchanged this for a Warship.

Southbound

A Stanier Cl.5 worked South to Weston on a local – the engine returning on a through service to the Midlands later – this train being followed by some ECS activities involving both steam and a DMU. Derby-Weston (train *1090*) arrived with a Peak which again worked through to return North later. A Weymouth Standard Cl.5 arrived – presumably from that town to be followed by 82XXX on a Bath Green Park service. A DMU worked a Bristol-Weston local before the arrival of three Paddington services and a Wolverhampton-Weston, these being in the hands of 6000 *King*

BRISTOL: By the time of this view, the Warships had already started their journeys to the scrap heap as had the North British Type 2s. The D95XX Class were already a thing of the past. Maroon stock had been replaced by blue and grey and soon the two-tone green of the Brush Type 4 would also be only a memory. The train is the 9.45 Paddington-Weston-super-Mare at Bathampton, 28th June,1969. *(Hugh Ballantyne)*

George V, 5934 *Kneller Hall,* 4082 *Windsor Castle* and 7012 *Barry Castle* respectively. Interspersed was an arrival from Weymouth with a Hall. A Stanier Class 5 worked in from Gloucester then a Castle (Paddington-Weston), 7301 (Bathampton-Weston) and D7018 (Paddington-Weston). In between 82004/36, 7815 *Fritwell Manor,* and a DMU arrived, the latter probably from Severn Beach and the first from Bath Green Park. A DMU departed for Taunton before the appearance of 44135 on ECS and D7040 on Paddington-Weston, D7015 being similarly employed one hour later. Of the other movements that day only the Bristol-Portishead (DMU), D845 *Sprightly* (Paddington-Weston) and 4131 on a freight could be identified.

It is unfortunate that so many of these arrivals could not be positively identified but

with the absence of both reporting numbers and a working timetable life could be difficult. The size of the station (then operating fifteen platforms) also made it impossible to "set off" in pursuit of the information as this only led to the observer missing other movements.

1963

A little more experience for the observer produced a more comprehensive survey.

The first item of note was the appearance of D63XX locomotives generally employed on ECS work. The Bristol-Bournemouth departed behind 41245 and Bristol-Gloucester with 73031.

Weston-Paddington services were all Hymek worked unless stated otherwise but the first Bristol-Weymouth was still worked by a Hall.

A County worked an unidentified ten coach train before a Hymek departed on Bristol-

Portsmouth. A Bristol-Westbury train was also Hymek worked with other services as in 1962.

Southbound steam was a little more active with a Castle on the lunchtime arrival from Paddington, going forward to Weston, 6319 on another Weston service, with a second Castle on the following train from Paddington. A Hall was provided for Trowbridge-Weston and 82XXX on Calne-Weston. Train *1187* – the teatime arrival from Paddington – was also in the hands of a Castle.

1964

The upgrading of diesel power started in 1964. The Bristol-Gloucester service went out behind a Peak whilst Weston-Paddington trains were now in the hands of Westerns in several cases, the rest being covered by Warships. One Weymouth diagram remained steam (this being a Southern Region responsibility) and the afternoon Bristol-Gloucester was a Standard Cl.5. The use of Standard Cl.4 76040 of Cricklewood to cover ECS work on the Midland side must have raised a few eyebrows – this type was rarely seen in the Bristol area.

Southbound workings were similar to the Northbound pattern but the arrival of a Brush Type 4 on a Salisbury-Bristol working was noteworthy.

1965

The only steam diagram to operate locally was that to Bath Green Park but even here a Hymek took one turn. A Tinsley Brush Type 4 worked out, probably to Westbury on the first recorded train, then appeared later on a Weymouth-Derby working. One Paddington service was also provided with a Brush Type 4.

Southbound also found Brush Type 4s employed on two services from Paddington. Weymouth services other than that above were DMU worked. It should be noted that D63XX had ceased activities at Bristol by this time.

January 1966 marked the end of Western Region steam. Future years would see the end of a steam practice – changing engines at Bristol – with Brush Type 4s and Peaks working throughout on services from the Midlands to the South West and the gradual demise of hydraulic power.

BRISTOL: On Summer Saturdays almost anything might be pressed into service on the Bristol-Birmingham line. Although recorded by the photographer at the time as a Paignton-Bradford relief, the IM20 reporting number would in fact suggest a Midland Region destination. This train did not run on the survey date in 1962 but did appear in 1963 (train *156*) when it ran to Derby behind a Blackpool Stanier Class 5 attached at Bristol. This view is taken at Lawrence Hill station with Hughes 2-6-0 42798 and it is almost certain that the train was routed via the Temple Meads avoiding line, engines being changed at St Philip's Marsh. 11th August 1962. *(B. W. L. Brooksbank)*

BRISTOL: The 1963 service V93 (09.30 Liverpool-Plymouth) was entrusted to second line motive power despite loading to twelve to fourteen carriages. 6836 *Estavarney Grange* is seen passing Horfield on 17th August. Three weeks earlier 6910 *Gossington Hall* did the honours (train *270*). *(Peter W. Gray)*

BRISTOL: A 'summer Saturday only' service was a through train from Carmarthen to Weston-super-Mare which produced a wide variety of motive power. 6957 *Norcliffe Hall* works through Horfield, on 17th August 1963. One of the GWR 'Ocean Liner' carriages is immediately behind the tender (see train *661*).

(Peter W. Gray)

P = Passing time

TABLE TWENTY-FIVE

SURVEY POINT: BRISTOL – NORTHBOUND – 28th JULY 1962

Train Ref. No.	Rep. No.	Time	Description	Motive power	Name	Allocation	Time Arr.	Time Dep.	Remarks
1049	B40		Bristol-Weymouth Town	4993	*Dalton Hall*	83C	09.30	09.40	Arrival E.C.S.
1050			Train not identified	DMU			09.40	09.47	
1051	IE68	09.10	Weston-super-Mare-Sheffield	44813		21A	09.44	09.50	
1052	IV65	06.45	Paignton-Bradford	45585	*Hyderbad*	15C		10.06	Arriving Engine/Time not recorded
1053	2		Train not identified	DMU				10.09	
1054	IA30	09.37	Weston-Super-Mare-Paddington	D7042		82A	10.15	10.21	
1055	2		Train not identified	DMU			10.49		
1056			Bristol-Portsmouth	4956	*Plowden Hall*	88A	10.50	10.52	Arrival E.C.S.
1057	B2		Bristol-Severn Beach	DMU				12.05	
1058			Bristol-Bath Green Park	82004		82F		12.10	
1059	IA50	11.35	Weston-super-Mare-Paddington	5963	*Wimpole Hall*	82D	12.14	12.17	
1060	2		Bristol-Bath Spa	DMU			12.27	12.30	Arrival ECS
1061	IV69	12.45	Bristol-Sheffield	45725	*Repulse*	41C	12.46	12.50	Gloucester times omitted from original records.
1062		12.15	Weston-super-Mare-Sheffield	45683	*Hogue*	41C	13.02	13.05	But see entry 892
1063			Bristol-Weymouth	73020		71G	13.04	13.10	Arrival ECS
1064		12.35	Weston-super-Mare-Paddington	5975	*Winslow Hall*	84B	13.10	13.20	
1065			Train not identified	73015		82E		13.36	
1066			Train not identified	4290		86A		13.45	Possibly E.C.S.
1067	B2		Train not identified	DMU			14.01	14.10	Possibly E.C.S.
1068			Train not identified	4248		87F	14.25		
1069		14.35	Weston-super-Mare-Paddington	6000	*King George V*	81A	15.05	15.15	
1070	2		Bristol-Weymouth	DMU				15.13	
1071			Train not identified	DMU				15.43	
1072	2B33		Bristol-Westbury?	D7017		82A	15.52	15.57	
1073			Bristol-Westbury	DMU			16.14	16.30	

TABLE TWENTY-FIVE (continued)

Train Ref. No.	Rep. No.	Time	Description	Motive power	Name	Allocation	Time Arr.	Time Dep.	Remarks
1074			-Bristol	DMU			16.20		Origin not established
1075	1V03		Bristol-Weymouth	6986	*Rydal Hall*	82C	16.40	17.00	
1076			Train not identified	4660		82B	16.52	17.03	
1077	2		Train not identified	DMU			17.10	17.20	
1078	1A16	16.35	Weston-super-Mare-Paddington	D868	*Zephyr*	83D	17.10	17.20	
1079			Bristol-	43963		21A		17.15	Train arrived behind D7018 (82A)
1080	2B11		Train not identified	D7000		82A	17.30	17.55	Probable destination Birmingham
1081	2		Bristol-Calne	DMU				17.35	Arrival E.C.S.
1082			Bristol-Severn Beach	DMU				18.06	
1083			Bristol-Bath Green Park	82007		82B		18.12	

TABLE TWENTY-SIX

SURVEY POINT: BRISTOL – SOUTHBOUND – 28th JULY 1962

Train Ref. No.	Rep. No.	Time	Description	Motive power	Name	Allocation	Arr.	Dep.	Remarks
1084	IV24		Bristol-Weston-super-Mare	44819		21A		09.41	Departure E.C.S.
1085			Train not identified	4956	*Plowden Hall*	88A	09.26	09.28	Stock for Bristol-Newcastle
1086			E.C.S.	41240		82F	09.41		Terminated
1087			Train not identified	DMU			09.56		
1088			Train not identified	82037		82B	10.29	10.35	
1089	2		Train not identified	DMU			10.45		Terminated
1090	IV28	06.40	Derby-Weston-super-Mare	D102		17A	10.51	10.58	
1091			Bristol-Taunton	DMU			10.55	11.01	Arrival not noted at Taunton
1092			Weymouth-Bristol	73029		71G	10.55	11.00	Departure E.C.S.
1093			Bath Green Park-Bristol	82004		82F	11.05		
1094	IB04	08.45	Paddington-Weston-super-Mare	6000	*King George V*	81A	11.19	11.21	
1095	B07		Paddington-Weston-super-Mare?	5934	*Kneller Hall*	82B	11.21	11.30	
1096	IB06	08.10	Wolverhampton-Weston-super-Mare	7012	*Barry Castle*	84A	11.30	11.32	
1097	IV03		Weymouth-Bristol	7901	*Dodington Hall*	82B	11.58		
1098		09.45	Paddington-Weston-super-Mare	4082	*Windsor Castle*	81A	12.43	13.00	
1099			Train not identified	4660		82B	12.50	13.05	
1100			Train not identified	4290		86A	13.05		
1101	2B74	11.50	Gloucester-Bristol	45006		21A	13.05		
1102		10.45	Paddington-Weston-super-Mare	5094	*Tretower Castle*	82B	13.40	13.50	
1103			Train not identified	DMU			13.46		
1104	2B96		Bathampton-Weston-super-Mare	7301		82B	14.00	14.10	
1105			Train not identified	82036		82B	14.10	14.20	
1107	IB13	11.45	Paddington-Weston-super-Mare	D7018		82A	14.40	14.55	
1108			Bath Green Park-Bristol	82004		82F	14.41		

TABLE TWENTY-SIX (continued)

Train Ref. No.	Rep. No.	Time	Description	Motive power	Name	Allocation	Time Arr.	Time Dep.	Remarks
1109	2		Severn Beach-Bristol	DMU			14.45		
1110			Train not identified	7815	Fritwell Manor	89C	15.05		
1111	6-44	12.45	Paddington-Weston-super-Mare	D7015		82A	15.20	15.40	
1112	2		Bristol-Taunton				16.15	16.30	
1113			E.C.S.	44135		82E	16.25		
1114	IC26	13.45	Paddington-Weston-super-Mare	D7040		82A	16.37	16.45	
1115			Train not identified	42790		21A	17.20	17.30	
1116	2		Bristol-Portishead	DMU			17.28	17.32	
1117	2		Severn Beach-Bristol	DMU			18.05		
1118			Train not identified	6936	Breccles Hall	88A	18.31		
1119			Freight	4131		82B		18p35	
1120		15.45	Paddington-Weston-super-Mare	D845	Sprightly	83A	18.37	19.01	

TABLE TWENTY-SEVEN

SURVEY POINT: BRISTOL – NORTHBOUND – 27th JULY 1963

P = Passing time

Train Ref. No.	Rep. No.	Time*	Description	Motive power	Name	Allocation	Arr.	Dep.	Remarks
1121			Train not identified	DMU				09.10	
1122	1B53		Bristol-Bournemouth	41245		82E		09.12	
1123			E.C.S.	D6352		82A		09.15	
1124			Bristol-Gloucester	73031		85C		09.15	
1125	1A20		Weston-super-Mare-Paddington	D70XX			09.16	09.20	
1126			E.C.S.	DMU			09.23		Arrival E.C.S.
1127	1B40		Bristol-Weymouth	5975	Winslow Hall	82B	09.30	09.43	
1128	1N63	06.45	Paignton-Bradford	61090		41F	09.50	10.05	Train arrived behind D863 (83D) & D7045 (82A)
1129	2B		E.C.S.	DMU			10.01		
1130	1A30	09.37	Weston-super-Mare-Paddington	D7028		82A	10.04	10.15	
1131			Parcels	3735		82D	10.22	10.36	
1132			Train not identified	1028	County of Warwick		10.25	10.39	
1133	1054		Bristol-Portsmouth	D7087		82B	10.36	10.57	
1134	1A42	10.40	Weston-super-Mare-Paddington	D7042		82A	11.06	11.15	
1135	1A50	11.35	Weston-super-Mare-Paddington	D7073		83A		12.15	
1136	B2		E.C.S.	DMU			12.05	12.09	
1137			Bristol-Bath Green Park	82004		82F	12.07	12.12	
1138	B2		E.C.S	DMU				12.30	
1139	H2		Bristol-Bath Spa	DMU				12.27	
1140	2B96		Train not identified	D6357		82A	12.33	12.39	
1141	B2		Bristol-Severn Beach	DMU				12.38	
1142	B2		Bristol-Gloucester	73028		82E		12.45	
1143	B2		Train not identified	DMU				13.02	
1144	434		Bristol-Weymouth	73080	Merlin	71G		13.09	
1145			Bristol-Gloucester	73091		85C		13.45	
1146			Bristol-Severn Beach	DMU				13.57	
1147			Freight	D6357		82A	14.14	14.22	

TABLE TWENTY-SEVEN (continued)

Train Ref. No.	Rep. No.	Time*	Description	Motive power	Name	Allocation	Arr.	Dep.	Remarks
1148			E.C.S.	61153		41A		15.05	
1149	IA74	14.35	Weston-super-Mare-Paddington	D7026		82A	15.07	15.26	
1150	B2		Bristol-Severn Beach	DMU				15.38	
1151	2B73		Bristol-Westbury -Bristol	D7025		82A	15.45	15.56	
1152	B2		Bristol	DMU			16.13		Origin not identified
1153			Bristol-Severn Beach	DMU				16.37	
1154	IX95		Train not identified	D7003		82A	16.52	17.01	
1155			Bristol-Bournemouth West	41207		82E		16.59	
1156	IA13	16.35	Weston-super-Mare-Paddington	D857	Undaunted	83D	17.07	17.15	Train arrived behind D7074 (82A)

* The 1963 Working Timetable was not available. Where the service was identical to that in 1962 the 1962 origin departure time is quoted.

TABLE TWENTY-EIGHT

SURVEY POINT: BRISTOL – SOUTHBOUND – 27th JULY 1963

P = Passing time

Train Ref. No.	Rep. No.	Time*	Description	Motive power	Name	Allocation	Arr.	Dep.	Remarks
1157			E.C.S.	DMU				09.11	
1158			E.C.S.	D6352				09.20	
1159	2B96		Bristol-Weston-super-Mare	D7070		82A	09.24	09.33	Arrival E.C.S.
1160	2B20		Cardiff-Bristol	D7087		88A	09.33	09.44	Departure E.C.S.
1161	B2		E.C.S.	DMU			09.45	10.05	
1162	B2		E.C.S.	DMU			09.48	09.49	
1163			E.C.S.	41208		82E	10.02		
1164	B2		E.C.S.	DMU			10.02	10.05	
1165	IV28	06.40	Derby-Weston-super-Mare	D147		17A	10.46	10.50	
1166			Bath Green Park-Bristol	82004		82F	1051	10.50	
1167	2B		-Bristol	DMU			10.58	11.05	Origin not known
1168	434	08.10	Weymouth-Bristol	73080	Merlin	71G	11.01	11.13	
1169	800		Wolverhampton-Weston-super-Mare	6842	Nunhold Grange	84F	11.06	11.10	
1170	2B		Bristol-Weston-super-Mare	DMU			11.14	11.50	
1171	IB04	08.45	Paddington-Weston-super-Mare	D7026		82A	11.21	11.26	Arrival E.C.S.
1172	B2		Severn Beach-Bristol	DMU			11.57		
1173	B2		Severn Beach-Bristol	DMU			12.32		
1174		09.45	Paddington-Weston-super-Mare	5056	Earl of Powis	81A	12.44	12.50	
1175	IB56		-Weston-super-Mare	6319		82D	12.49	12.55	Origin not established
1176			Bath Green Park-Bristol	41208		82E	13.15		
1177		10.45	Paddington-Weston-super-Mare	7036	Taunton Castle	81A	13.16	13.28	
1178			Trowbridge-Weston-super-Mare	6924	Grantley Hall	81D	13.39	13.50	
1179			Gloucester-Bristol	61153		41A	14.08		
1180		13.12	Calne-Weston-super-Mare	82035		82E	14.12	14.20	
1181	IC80	11.45	Paddington-Weston-super-Mare	D7074		82A	14.31	14.40	
1182			Bath Green Park-Bristol	82004		82F	14.45		

TABLE TWENTY-EIGHT (continued)

Train Ref. No.	Rep. No.	Time*	Description	Motive power	Name	Allocation	Time Arr.	Dep.	Remarks
1183	2B		Severn Beach-Bristol	DMU			14.47		
1184			Salisbury-Bristol	6982	*Melmerby Hall*	82B	15.03		
1185			Severn Beach-Bristol	DMU			15.17		
1186	IB15	12.45	Paddington-Weston-super-Mare	D7044		82A	15.20	15.30	
1187	IB17	13.45	Paddington-Weston-super-Mare	7010	*Avondale Castle*	81A	16.34	16.45	
1188	B2		Train not identified	DMU			16.48		
1189	B2		Train not identified	DMU			17.00		
1190			Bournemouth-Bristol	41245		82E	17.11		
1191	B2		Bristol-Weston-super-Mare	DMU				17.32	

TABLE TWENTY-NINE

SURVEY POINT: BRISTOL – NORTHBOUND – 25th JULY 1964

P = Passing time

Train Ref. No.	Rep. No.	Time*	Description	Motive power	Name	Allocation	Arr.	Dep.	Remarks
1192	3B9		E.C.S.	D6351		82A		09.00	
1193	B2		Bristol-Severn Beach	DMU				09.04	
1194	IA20	08.35	Weston-super-Mare-Paddington	D1020	Western Hero	82A	09.06	09.15	
1195			E.C.S.	82037		82E		09.07	
1196	2D74		Bristol-Gloucester	D118		16C		09.16	
1197			E.C.S.	76040		14B		09.18	
1198	6F97		Bristol-Weymouth	D7023		82A	09.30	09.43	
1199	B2		E.C.S.	DMU				09.50	
1200	IA26	09.40	Weston-super-Mare-Paddington	D852	Tenacious	84A	10.03	10.15	
1201	1054		Bristol-Portsmouth	D7087		86A	10.31	10.54	
1202			Parcels	82004		82F		11p00	
1203	IA32	10.35	Weston-super-Mare-Paddington	D1024	Western Huntsman	86A	11.09	11.20	
1204	B2		Bristol-Severn Beach	DMU			11.40	12.06	Arrival E.C.S.
1205	IA40	11.35	Weston-super-Mare-Paddington	D832	Onslaught	83A	12.11	12.19	
1206			Bristol-Bath Green Park	82004		82F		12.13	
1207	B2		Bristol-Severn Beach	DMU				12.23	
1208			Bristol-Weymouth	73080	Merlin	71G	12.46	13.07	
1209	B2		Bristol-Severn Beach	DMU				13.02	
1210	IA30	12.35	Weston-super-Mare-Paddington	D828	Magnificent	83A	13.13	13.17	
1211			Bristol-Gloucester	73091		85C		13.31	
1212			Freight	D6354		82A	13.45	14.25	
1213			E.C.S.	82001		82E		14.07	
1214	B2		Bristol-Severn Beach	DMU				14.10	
1215	IN97		E.C.S.	76040		14B		15.00	
1216	B2		Bristol-Severn Beach	DMU				15.02	
1217	B2		Bristol-Weymouth	DMU				15.06	

TABLE TWENTY-NINE (continued)

Train Ref. No.	Rep. No.	Time*	Description	Motive power	Name	Allocation	Time Arr.	Time Dep.	Remarks
1218	IA66	14.35	Weston-super-Mare-Paddington	D1007	*Western Talisman*	86A	15.12	15.20	
1219	B2		Bristol-Severn Beach	DMU				15.23	
1220			Bristol-Bath Green Park	82004		82F		15.31	
1221	IC73		Bristol-Salisbury	D7075		82A	15.42	15.56	
1222	B2		E.C.S.	DMU				15.58	Arrival E.C.S.

TABLE THIRTY

SURVEY POINT: BRISTOL – SOUTHBOUND – 25th JULY 1964

Train Ref. No.	Rep. No.	Time	Description	Motive power	Name	Allocation	Arr.	Dep.	Remarks
1223			Parcels	D7019		82A	09.01	13.05	
1224	2B20	09.15	Bristol-Weston-super-Mare	61394		41F		09.15	Departure E.C.S.
1225	2B		Westbury-Bristol	D7087		82	09.26	09.38	Trains combined and
1226	B2		-Bristol	DMU			09.48		departed E.C.S.
1227			-Bristol	DMU			09.52	09.58	
1228			E.C.S.	82001		82E	10.03		
1229	IB04	07.45	Paddington-Weston-super-Mare	D828	Magnificent	83A	10.16	10.30	
1230			Parcels ex Derby	44810		2E		10p25	
1231	IV28		Derby-Weston-super-Mare	D99	3rd Caribinier	16C	10.31	10.40	
1232			Severn Beach-Bristol	DMU			10.49		
1233			Bath Green Park-Bristol	82004		82F	10.51		
1234			Bristol-Weymouth	73080	Merlin	71G	10.54	11.00	
1235	IB06	08.45	Paddington-Weston-super-Mare (Locking Road)						Departure E.C.S.
1236	V56		Wolverhampton-Weston-super-Mare	D860	Victorious	84A	11.00	11.23	
1237			Weston-super-Mare	6848	Toddington Grange	85A	11.06	11.10	
1238			Train not identified	DMU			11.30		
			Freight	92238		82E		11p46	
1239	IB08	09.45	Paddington-Weston-super-Mare	D857	Undaunted	84A	12.35	12.45	
1240	B2		Severn Beach-Bristol	DMU			12.37		
1241	IB10	10.45	Paddington-Weston-super-Mare						
1242	2B96		Weston-super-Mare	D1007	Western Talisman	86A	12.55	13.10	
1243	B2		Train not identified	D7041		82A	13.00	13.12	
1244	2B78		Severn Beach-Bristol	DMU			13.56		
			Gloucester-Bristol	D118		16C	14.00		
1245		14.18	Bristol-Weston-super-Mare (Locking Road)	82036		82E	14.08	14.20	Arrival E.C.S.

TABLE THIRTY (continued)

Train Ref. No.	Rep. No.	Time	Description	Motive power	Name	Allocation	Time Arr.	Dep.	Remarks
1246			E.C.S.	76040		14B	14.08		
1247			Salisbury-Bristol	73012		87F	14.13		
1248	IB13	11.45	Paddington-Weston-super-Mare	D1000	*Western Enterprise*	81A	14.17	14.34	
1249			Bath Green Park-Bristol	82004		82F	14.37		
1250	B2		Severn Beach-Bristol	DMU			14.46		
1251	2B70		Salisbury-Bristol	D1742		?	15.05		
1252	IB15	12.45	Paddington-Weston-super-Mare	D1020	*Western Hero*	82A	15.10	15.26	
1253	B2		Train not identified	DMU			15.33		
1254	9C03		Freight	D6354		82A		16p00	
1255	B2		Severn Beach-Bristol	DMU			16.17		
1256	IB17	13.45	Paddington-Weston-super-Mare	D867	*Zenith*	84A	16.19	16.25	

TABLE THIRTY-ONE

SURVEY POINT: BRISTOL – NORTHBOUND – 21st AUGUST 1965

P = Passing time

Train Ref. No.	Rep. No.	Time	Description	Motive power	Name	Allocation	Time Arr.	Dep.	Remarks
1257	1053	09.00	Bristol-Weymouth	D1872		41A		09.00	
1258	IA22	08.30	Weston-super-Mare-Paddington	D1021	*Western Cavalier*	82A	09.05	09.17	
1259	B2	09.12	Bristol T.M.-Severn Beach	DMU				09.12	
1260	2C93	09.00	Bristol T.M.-Bournemouth	D1589		87E		09.13	
1261			Freight	82001		82E		09p22	
1262		09.35	Bristol-Newcastle	D41		82A		09.36	
1263		10.05	Bristol-Weymouth	DMU			09.44	10.05	Arrival E.C.S.
1264			Bristol-Severn Beach	DMU				10.00	
1265	IA25	09.40	Weston-super-Mare-Paddington	D1057	*Western Chieftain*	87E	10.04	10.14	
1266	B2	10.20	Bristol-Severn Beach	DMU				10.00	
1267	B2	10.55	Bristol-Weymouth	DMU			10.34	10.55	Arrival E.C.S.
1268	IA34	10.35	Weston-super-Mare-Paddington	D1043	*Western Duke*	82A	11.06	11.16	
1269			Train not identified	DMU			11.45	11.56	
1270		12.10	Bristol-Bath Green Park	82001		82E		12.12	
1271	B2	12.25	Bristol-Bath Spa	DMU			12.20	12.35	Arrival E.C.S.
1272			Train not identified	DMU			12.24	12.57	
1273	IA50	12.35	Weston-super-Mare-Paddington	D867	*Zenith*	84A	13.00	13.18	
1274 each	DMU	13.02	Bristol-Severn B116			13.05			
1275			Train not identified	DMU				13.21	
1276	B2	14.02	Bristol-Severn Beach	DMU				14.02	
1277	IA02	14.40	Weston-super-Mare-Paddington	D1001	*Western Pathfinder*	84A	15.05	15.16	
1278	B2	15.12	Bristol-Severn Beach	DMU				15.13	
1279		15.35	Bristol-Bath Green Park	82004		82F		15.40	

TABLE THIRTY-ONE (continued)

Train Ref. No.	Rep. No.	Time	Description	Motive power	Name	Allocation	Time Arr.	Dep.	Remarks
1280		14.50	Taunton-Bristol	DMU			16.05	16.13	Train not recorded at Taunton, departure E.C.S.
1281		16.30	Bristol-Westbury	DMU				16.32	
1282	IT33	16.52	Bristol-Bath Green Park E.C.S.	D7002		82A	16.39	16.55	Arrival E.C.S.
1283				DMU				16.42	
1284	B2	16.53	Bristol-Severn Beach	DMU				16.55	
1285	IA02	16.35	Weston-super-Mare-Paddington	D1712		82A	17.11	17.19	
1286		17.10	Weston-super-Mare-Bath Spa	D7004		82A	17.51	17.58	

TABLE THIRTY-TWO

SURVEY POINT: BRISTOL – SOUTHBOUND – 21st AUGUST 1965

Train Ref. No.	Rep. No.	Time	Description	Motive power	Name	Allocation	Time Arr.	Time Dep.	Remarks
1287	B2	08.21	Severn Beach-Bristol	DMU			09.02		
1288	2B96	09.10	Bristol-Weston-super-Mare	D1597		82A	09.06	09.10	Arrival E.C.S.
1289	IV30	06.10	Derby-Weymouth	D1720		82A	09.40	09.50	Train arrived behind D117 (ML)
1290		08.42	Chippenham-Bristol				09.54	10.02	Departure E.C.S.
1291	B2	09.10	Severn Beach-Bristol				09.55		
1292	2V14	02.00	Derby-Bristol Parcels	D59	*Royal Warwickshire Regiment*	ML	09.58	10.05	
1293	IB04	07.45	Paddington-Weston-super-Mare	D867	*Zenith*	84A	10.10	10.25	
1294	IB06	08.45	Paddington-Weston-super-Mare	D1727		81A	10.38	10.54	
1295		10.10	Bath Green Park-Bristol	82004		82F	10.48		
1296		08.51	Weymouth-Bristol	DMU			11.20	11.29	Departure E.C.S.
1297	IV31	07.35	Sheffield-Bristol	D25		55A	11.31		
1298	2B96	11.55	Bristol-Weston-super-Mare	D7004		82A	11.37	11.55	Arrival E.C.S.
1299		11.14	Bath Spa-Bristol	DMU			11.39	11.40	Departure E.C.S.
1300		11.08	Severn Beach-Bristol	DMU			12.03		
1301	IB08	09.45	Paddington-Weston-super-Mare	D1010	*Western Campaigner*	84A	12.13	12.32	
1302	IB10	10.45	Paddington-Weston-super-Mare	D1001	*Western Pathfinder*	84A	12.54	13.07	
1303	3M32	12.25	Bath Green Park-Bristol	D1589		87E	13.06		
1304		12.15	Severn Beach-Bristol	DMU			13.08		
1305		13.10	Bath Spa-Bristol	DMU			13.34		
1306	2B96	13.00	Swindon-Weston-super-Mare	D7014		82A	14.10	14.35	
1307	IK44	11.45	Paddington-Weston-super-Mare	D1712		82A	14.19	14.30	
1308			Train not identified	DMU			14.22		

TABLE THIRTY-TWO (continued)

Train Ref. No.	Rep. No.	Time	Description	Motive power	Name	Allocation	Time Arr.	Time Dep.	Remarks
1309	B2	14.00	Severn Beach–Bristol	DMU			14.43		
1310		14.10	Bath Green Park–Bristol	82004		82F	14.46		
1311	IB15	12.45	Paddington–Weston-super-Mare	D1051	Western Ambassador	84A	14.59	15.09	
1312	B2	12.56	Weymouth–Bristol	DMU			15.34	15.41	Departure E.C.S.
1313	B2	14.55	Severn Beach–Bristol	DMU			15.41		
1314		16.30	Bristol–Taunton	DMU			16.01	16.30	Departure E.C.S., train not recorded at Taunton
1315	IB17	13.45	Paddington–Weston-super-Mare	D1021	Western Cavalier	82A	16.04	16.20	
1316	2B54		E.C.S.	DMU			16.44	17.05	
1317	B2	16.00	Severn Beach–Bristol	DMU			16.44		
1318		16.30	Bath Green Park–Bristol	82001		82E	17.10		

BRISTOL: B1 61327 (41D) stands under the vast roof of Bristol Temple Meads platform nine on 27th June 1964. Train reporting number 1N48 confirms that the train is 09.00 Paignton-Leeds which on 25th July 1964 was provided with a Newton Heath Jubilee (train *291*). *(Peter W. Gray)*

BRISTOL: A regular 'out and back' working for an Oxley Castle in 1964 involved the 06.35 Wolverhampton-Paignton and 11.20 Newquay-Wolverhampton to/from Bristol. 7012 *Barry Castle* was in charge for the return on 1st August at Wickwar. One week earlier it was 5063 *Earl Baldwin* (train *331*). *(Peter W. Gray)*

BRISTOL: How quickly the scene could change. Four weeks after this view was taken a Class 47 had charge of this turn, the 12.17 Minehead and Ilfracombe to Wolverhampton (train *433*). Here 6918 *Sandon Hall* devoid of name and cabside number plates storms through Lawrence Hill station. In the early part of the 1965 Summer timetable the Wolverhampton services produced the only steam hauled main line trains from Bristol. 31st July 1965. *(B. W. L. Brooksbank)*

BRISTOL: Double heading was not common but at the start and end of the Summer timetable there were some unbalanced workings. Hymeks D7023 and D7025 have just arrived at Bristol Temple Meads on IV48 09.00 Paignton-Sheffield (see train *158*). 29th June 1963. *(J. H. Sparkes)*

BRISTOL: Super power was provided for this Midlands bound express at Bristol Temple Meads on 18th September 1967. Early design 'Warship' D604 *Cossack* leads 'Western' D1057 *Western Chieftain. (Terry Nicholls)*

BRISTOL: Changes at the North end of Bristol Temple Meads – Paddington trains used to leave from the right-hand platform where Peak 45049 *The Staffordshire Regiment (The Prince of Wales's)* stands on 9.33 Penzance-Wolverhampton. This train had arrived behind shunter 08935 hauling 47080 that had failed in the Bristol suburbs. HST set 253008 is working the 14.38 Weston-Paddington. The Post Office bridge is very evident in this view. July 7th 1979. *(Michael Mensing)*

8. Services around Weston-super-Mare – a closer look

In this chapter the transition from steam to diesel over a five year period is charted with a look at the levels of steam and diesel activity as well as some of the more unusual engines to put in an appearance on the local scene.

Although the observations are for one area a similar picture could be seen at numerous locations across our railway system in the 1960s.

Observations quoted were taken at Worle Junction which is located about two miles North from Weston-super-Mare and is the point at which the loop line serving Weston diverges from the main Bristol-Taunton line, the two merging again South of Weston at Uphill Junction. At this time Weston used to boast two stations – General and Locking Road, the latter being a four platform dead end station used mainly for excursion traffic but used also on Summer Saturdays for the "morning Northbound rush."

8.1 Winter Timetable Services

The first real effects of dieselisation started to be seen in the Winter of 1960/1961 as one at a time major cross country trains changed to diesel power. DMUs had for some time been working the local services in the Winter. It maybe worthwhile reminding readers that 30 years ago the number of through cross country services were much less than today during the winter period. Due to this lack of "interesting trains" observations tended to be confined to Saturday mornings only – a

WESTON-SUPER-MARE: Unfortunately not captured at Weston, but at Severn Tunnel Junction, the Liverpool-Plymouth express which ran throughout the year, was the last regular through steam working and in fact was a "lodging turn" for Newton Abbot and Shrewsbury crews. The engines also worked through between those points and the competition for cleanliness was immense, the latest ex-works engine always being allocated, usually a Castle from Newton Abbot, but frequently a County from Shrewsbury or even a Hall. Warships were substituted and worked throughout as the steam engines had done – briefly continuing as far as Crewe. However with the coming of the Class 47s, engine changing started to take place at Bristol. In later years these services were routed via Birmingham. 5059 *Earl St. Aldwyn,* July 1961. *(J. Champion)*

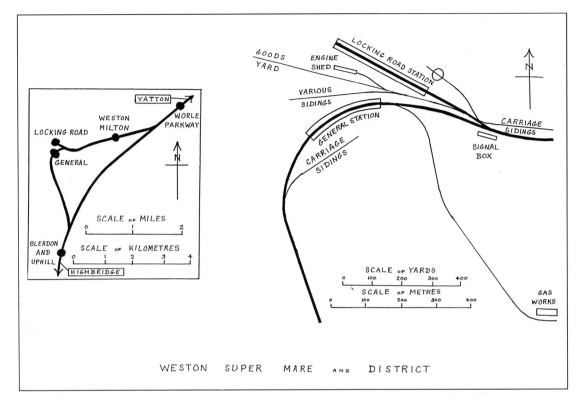

WESTON SUPER MARE ᴀɴᴅ DISTRICT

midweek trainspotter was almost unheard of in those days.

The main traffic flows consisted of services to Paddington (from Weston) and South-West to South Wales, the North West and the Midlands (two or three trains only per day, these however being ten to fourteen coach trains of major importance).

In steam days the Paddington trains frequently had a local Hall on the Weston-Bristol leg thus allowing the incoming Castle to remain at Bristol for servicing. By the Winter of 1961/2 Warships had taken over most duties and these ran through to Weston. *The Devonian* (Paignton-Bradford) had also succumbed to Warship haulage along with the Plymouth-Cardiff (as far as Bristol). North British Warships also appeared at random (e.g. D600 *Active* on 12.00 noon Penzance-Crewe on 23rd September 1961).

The one major service still in the hands of steam was 08.00 Plymouth-Manchester and Liverpool (1M91) and the corresponding 09.10 from Manchester (1V93). This was what was known as a lodging turn with the crew

(and engine) working through from Newton Abbot to Shrewsbury on Day 1 returning on Day 2. There was great competition between the two depots to see who could turnout the cleanest engine and the engine most recently out of works was usually provided (at least from Shrewsbury) using a County or Castle. During the course of a Saturday morning up to six freights could be recorded, all steam hauled, Halls and 28XX being the favourite power.

The Plymouth-Manchester service went over to diesel haulage in week commencing 5th March 1962. Occasional diesel failures or shortages brought steam back into action such as the appearance of 7909 *Heveningham Hall* on the down *Devonian* on 31st March 1962.

As the 1962 Summer timetable came nearer some additional services were run and the survey times expanded but steam numbers actually fell as freight started to go over to diesel power. The first Hymeks were in evidence on these services and the number of Warships available expanded rapidly. The first recorded Western (D1001 *Western Pathfinder*)

WESTON-SUPER-MARE: Warship D831 *Monarch* in "as delivered" condition is seen heading south from Weston-super-Mare on a midweek service, the reporting number apparently being incorrect, as all "B" services terminated in the Bristol area. The next possible destination would be Taunton in the "C" (Exeter) area. 4th July 1962. *(Michael Mensing)*

worked through on 22nd April 1962 on 11.08 Plymouth-Cardiff.

One of the last Saturdays before the new timetable – 9th June 1962 produced the following interesting observations.

D604 *Cossack* worked through on thirteen coaches with 1C20 Paddington-Plymouth, (09.01) 4992 *Crosby Hall* and 5954 *Faendre Hall* both worked North with ECS (09.25 and 09.37) whilst 5946 *Marwell Hall* went South with an extra to Penzance (10.10).

An extra Southbound service with Castle 5052 *Earl of Radnor* included one pair of Midland articulated coaches whilst the following Cardiff-Weston DMU included an additional Hawksworth designed coach in its formation. Steam covered several other "extras" but D1004 *Western Crusader* passed at 14.13 on 17.30 Plymouth-Cardiff whilst a steam diesel double header (D824 *Highflyer*/6814 *Enbourne Grange*) went South at 15.38.

As surely as diesel replaces steam, the Summer soon passed and the Winter

timetable returned. Steam became confined to, on average, two/three freights only, again with a 28XX or Hall generally in charge, although 6320 of Severn Tunnel Junction appeared on 20th October. Diesel shortages also continued – this being the time when the Westerns were at their most problematical and Castle 5071 *Spitfire* deputised on the Cardiff-Plymouth on the same date. At this time the Paxman engined Warship D830 *Majestic* had a regular duty on *The Devonian*.

Those readers with long memories will recall that the Winter of 1962/63 was extremely harsh – even in Somerset. Snow started falling around the end of December and was still on the ground in early March. Unfortunately the average young spotter of the day was not sufficiently hardy to brave the icy blast on a railway bridge for three-four hours to see what he thought was the never ending stream of diesels. On venturing out in mid February it was to find a transformed world. Of fifteen trains seen on 16th February, seven were steam hauled with 6936 *Beccles Hall*

WESTON-SUPER-MARE: The 10.00 Exeter-Manchester headed by 6934 *Beachamwell Hall* is seen between Uphill Junction and Weston-super-Mare General. In the survey (train *011*) this was a Warship working so it is possible that diesels were in short supply on this day in June 1962. *(Michael Mensing)*

(Cardiff) on the early Taunton-Paddington, 6863 *Dolhywel Grange* of Reading on the prestigious Plymouth-Glasgow and 6981 *Marbury Hall* of St. Philip's Marsh on the Cardiff-Plymouth. Freights were handled by 6913 *Levens Hall*, 6954 *Lotherton Hall*, 6833 *Calcot Grange* and 3677 (But D830 *Majestic* was on its regular turn!).

23rd February – fifteen trains, seven steam again – the Plymouth-Glasgow was back to diesel but the 11.40 Paddington was Castle hauled – and D830 was on *The Devonian*.

2nd March – fourteen trains – seven steam including Cardiff-Plymouth (6863 again) and Weston-Paddington (6966 *Withingham Hall*). No prizes for guessing what D830 was working!

After that the weather must have taken a turn for the worse (probably rain!) because it was 23rd March before the next observations and there were signs of normality returning

although steam was still to be seen on two passenger turns. D830 however must have been indisposed – but it was back in the harness on 2nd April.

A stranger seen on this date was 2-8-2 tank 7249 of Severn Tunnel Junction on a Southbound freight. No Westerns were recorded until the beginning of June on these Saturday observations. Hymeks also were seen only in twos and threes and yet as we saw earlier in the Summer they were hauling up to 50% of services.

25th May 1963 was a typical pre-Summer service day with a few steam engines working freight duties – seen on passenger work was 45584 *North West Frontier* of Derby which arrived on a Midland line special in mid morning. At this time Weston used to boast a diesel shunter as pilot and D4024 came South in mid-afternoon for this duty. Pre-nationalisation coaching stock was commonly

BRISTOL: The Western approaches to Temple Meads station on 3rd March 1974 showing the contemporary operational scene – all blue Cl.47s on expresses and blue and grey first generation dmus on local and intermediate (pictured) services. Bath Road shed yard is rear, right with 2xCl.47. A 'Peak' is in the station. *(Terry Nicholls)*

seen. The fifteen coach IM91 included two GWR, one LNER and one LMS vehicle in its formation, IB10 Paddington-Weston, one GWR and IV92 relief to Paignton was composed of one LNER and nine LMS coaches.

The standard DMUs of the time were the Swindon designs plus some of the Derby types. Pressed steel units occasionally worked through from Plymouth. Of note on 1st June 1963 was the inclusion of single unit W55033 and trailer in the formation of a midday Bristol-Taunton working.

The 1963-4 Winter service started as the previous service finished – a few steam movements almost exclusively on freight work, Warships (but by now only the D800 variety) were in charge of most of the other trains

interspersed with Hymeks and DMUs. Westerns were not in evidence, their previous working (Plymouth-Cardiff) was now in the hands of the latest four-car Swindon-built DMUs.

19th October saw the passage of *Flying Scotsman* on a Paddington-Ilfracombe and return working.

In October a disproportionate number of steam appearances were in the hands of Counties:–

12th	1000	*County of Middlesex*
	1014	*County of Glamorgan*
	1021	*County of Montgomery.*
19th	1000	*County of Middlesex*
	1021	*County of Montgomery,*
	1028	*County of Warwick*
26th	1020	*County of Monmouth.*

In late November a diesel shortage must have developed as no fewer than five steam engines appeared in the morning session of which 4920 *Dumbleton Hall* was on a Taunton-Paddington duty and both the Weston-Paddington turns were entrusted to Hymeks.

On 7th December the morning was brightened by the appearance of Saltley Cl.9F – 92137. D830 *Majestic* must have either been out of service on other duties – it was not recorded until working up light on 28th December.

A sign of things to come was the appearance on 3rd January 1964 of D1689 on driver training duties, the Taunton-Paddington duty however was worked by 4082 *Windsor Castle* on this date, D7000 on 4th January but by 6974 *Bryngwyn Hall* on 11th. On this date only two trains were worked by Warships with seven Hymeks and five steam with three DMUs.

By March a degree of normality was restored with steam confined to freight duties. Two changes had taken place with diesel power – the Cardiff-Plymouth trains had become a Hymek duty (usually a Canton based example) and the 11.40 Weston-Paddington was in the hands of a Western – there now being a handful allocated to Bristol. The Brush Type 4 test train was running again but only on a Monday-Friday basis and workings by Westerns were becoming more commonplace with, on average, three appearing daily. Included in a Northbound freight on 11th April was a withdrawn Ivatt tank, 41276, the train being headed by D7020.

The final Saturday before the start of the Summer timetable (13th June) produced the following tally of movements from an observation period of 09.20 to 19.25 with an hour's break each for lunch and tea.

DMU 11, Warship 21, Western 9, Hymek 13, Steam 6 – (2 light engines and the inward and return legs of two excursions).

The Winter timetable of 1964/65 reduced the regular steam working to the 07.58 Bristol West Depot-Weston freight with the locomotive returning light to Barrow Road at 12.05 having carried out any necessary shunting at Weston. This duty was covered by virtually anything of Great Western origin available, from Pannier Tanks to Halls.

The variability of observations was considerable, e.g. on 7th November the tally

During the changeover period Hymeks abounded on freight turns replacing Halls, Granges and 2-8-0s. Front line steam was also cascaded from top link work to fast freight turns to allow further freight and mixed traffic steam stock withdrawals whilst facilitating front line deputation for diesel failures. 5029 *Nunney Castle* passes D7002 on 26th January 1963 at Patchway. *(Terry Nicholls)*

WESTON-SUPER-MARE: From the end of the 1960s Warship operation of mainly long distance services was superseded by Peak Type 4s, examples from all depots working right through into the West Country. From the headcode displayed in this view taken at Worle Junction D28 of Holbeck appears to be working a Western Region internal service.

(Author's Collection)

of movements produced 2 DMU, 3 Warships, 6 Westerns (5 on freights), 8 Hymeks and 2 steam whilst on 21st November the score was 2 DMU, 5 Warships, 1 Western, 12 Hymeks and 2 steam. The Plymouth-Cardiff workings had reverted to DMUs for this timetable.

On 6th March Barrow Road must have run out of GWR power, as the engine provided for the local freight was Stanier Cl.8F 48000. 3rd April 1965 provided a few interesting movements. D1028 *Western Hussar* worked up with 06.55 Plymouth-Liverpool followed by D1043 *Western Duke* on the 09.40 Weston-Paddington (in previous years the service started from Taunton) and then D7088 (ex works) on IX26 special to Wembley. The Taunton local was now provided by a 09.26 Taunton-Weymouth through service (DMU). At 10.50 a parcels train proceeded down the main line headed by D9504 this locomotive returning light at 12.22. On this day D830 *Majestic* was again rostered to the Paignton-Bradford but on both the preceding and

following Saturdays the train was in the hands of a Western. Final workings were a surprise appearance of Exmouth Junction's 75025 on a breakdown train and another through DMU turn 12.06 Bristol-Minehead.

When the 1965/66 Winter timetable began all steam activity had ceased. A marked drop in the number of Hymeks was recorded as Western and then Brush Type 4 appearances increased.

On Thursday April 11th 1966 the picture was Warship 7, Western 4, Brush Type 4 3, Hymek 2.

8.2 Summer Timetable Services

Observations in Summer in the Weston area were an altogether different affair to Winter with, on Saturdays, the large number of extra services between the South West and South Wales, the North-West and Midlands many of which bypassed Weston via the main line. In addition however the volume of holiday business generated at Weston warranted additional trains starting from Weston together with the extension of some services normally terminating at Bristol. Both during the week and mainly on Sundays rather than Saturdays there were also day excursions to Weston.

The Summer service of 1961 probably looked little different from that of the preceding ten years. Most of the work was performed by steam engines and the main interest lay in seeing how many rare engines would appear.

As set out in preceding chapters the succession of Halls, Granges and Castles was broken only occasionally by a Warship, possibly five or six being observed in a "full day".

So what might "catch the eye" in 1961?

There were two diagrams bringing Midland or Eastern Region engines to Weston – firstly a local turn from Bristol returning with the 12.04 Weston (Locking Road)-Sheffield and secondly on 06.40 Derby-Weston. Normal motive power for the former was a Jubilee from either Barrow Road or the Sheffield area whilst a Saltley Stanier Cl.5 worked the Derby service. On 1st July a Holbeck Jubilee (45569 *Tasmania*) appeared on the former also working on 15th July, whilst Patriot 45532 *Illustrious* of Nottingham seemed to be a late substitute on 29th July. 73065 was noted on 9th September.

A Southern Region Standard Cl.5 also reached Weston regularly. The Weymouth engine worked in on 13.52 Bristol-Weston-super-Mare returning on 19.30 Weston-Bristol. Another standard type that might appear was a Canton based Britannia – possibly one per two weeks.

Kings were extremely rare although 6016 *King Edward V* did work as a diesel substitute on IM99 Penzance-Glasgow Mail on 22nd July. Only one Manor was seen by the observer during the whole Summer, this being 7823 *Hook Norton Manor* on 10.12 Ilfracombe-Wolverhampton on 2nd September.

An occasional 47XX was to be expected but a definite "one-off" was the appearance of 92007 of Newport on 09.50 Carmarthen-Weston on 22nd July.

GWR origin oddities were 5913 *Rushton Hall* (Landore) on 09.05 Paignton-Manchester (17th June), 4935 *Ketley Hall* (Carmarthen)

07.45 Paignton-Newcastle (1st July), 7307 (Llanelli) 07.30 Blaina-Weston (Locking Road) 22nd July, 5953 *Dunley Hall* (Carmarthen) on 09.05 Bradford-Paignton on 2nd September and 5649 (Tondu) with a twelve coach special 19.15 Weston-Bridgend (2nd September).

A Toton Cl.8F - 48530 - worked a freight South on 1st July.

1962, as we have seen, brought the widespread use of Hymeks on the Summer extras these being almost exclusively Bath Road examples. With all the Warships being allocated to either Newton Abbot or Laira, there was in theory no rare Warship at Weston with about twenty workings being covered by the class. DMUs were notable by their absence only two or three diagrams being so worked between 09.00 and 19.00. There were no diagrams for Westerns on Summer Saturdays.

The Derby-Weston service became Peak operated, whilst the Sheffield train tended to be rostered to a Saltley Stanier Cl.5, or a Sheffield Jubilee. The Weymouth Standard Cl.5 did not appear, this being replaced by a Bathampton-Weston service with WR motive power.

Kings were (in their last season) more common with the diagram from Paddington arriving around noon, returning at 14.35, being the one most likely to be so worked. On some Saturdays two Kings were seen. A regular turn for an 82XXX tank was introduced via the Calne-Weston service arriving around 15.00. 4935 *Ketley Hall,* a Didcot Hall was a stranger on Wolverhampton-Penzance on 30th June, and the same date produced 4701/4 both on freights whilst on 14th July 4706 headed a Minehead-Cardiff. 92083 of Leicester was a stranger on this date in charge of the Plymouth parcels going south in late afternoon.

A spectacle of this summer service was the triple headed Southbound light engine movement around 09.30, the locomotives being used to work the 10.40, 11.40 and 12.40 services to Paddington – usually two Castles and a Hall or a County.

On 4th August the Weston-Sheffield ran in two parts, 45570 *New Zealand* leaving ahead of Patriot 45536 *Private W. Wood, V.C.* both 41A. 11th August found super power on the second turn with the provision of Royal Scot 46164 *The Artist's Rifleman*.

The overall balance of diesel to steam was about 60:40. 1962 saw fewer South Wales based steam engines on duty and no Manors were recorded.

The 1963 summer service opened on 22nd June. The overall level of service remained as in 1962 with little variations here and there. An early service was a Paddington-Minehead train which was in Weston by 09.25. This became a regular duty for an Old Oak Common allocated Hymek, usually the only London-based example seen during the day (or week). In total around forty of the day's movements were in the hands of Hymeks, Bath Road providing most of these. There were, however, occasional appearances by Canton Hymeks, and IM90 Exmouth-Manchester was a regular diagram for a Newton Abbot example. The level of Warship activity was a little higher than the previous year, but Westerns again were scarce covering only a few Paddington turns. A diagram for a Derby based Peak continued as in 1962 for the first Saturday only. In addition to the steam duties identified in the main Taunton survey section the following provided fairly regular activity – IF19 Weston-Swansea, IA50 Weston-Paddington, Paddington-Weston (14.00 arrival), Trowbridge-Weston, Derby-Weston returning on Weston-Sheffield, Carmarthen-Weston, Calne-Weston.

To see what the "competition" was up to, 29th June 1963 was chosen for a survey at Exeter Central. Western influence was just being brought to bear with the use of D63XX locomotives on Plymouth-Exeter services via the Southern Region route. Five of these machines were seen in an eight-hour period – all other trains were still steam worked mainly by Bulleid Pacifics but with the help of S15, U and N classes as well as Standard and Ivatt tanks with W class 31911/4 providing banking services.

Returning to the Western main line, let us consider the season's strangers. Where steam was employed from Paddington this was almost always a Castle either from Old Oak or Reading. On the first Saturday there must have been some diesel problems as both IM91 Penzance-Liverpool and the last Newquay-

Wolverhampton were hauled by Castles – this not being repeated during the season. An "old stager" which made regular appearances on freight traffic was 2822 from Taunton this being almost the oldest steam power in service on the WR.

The Derby-Weston turn provided an extremely tight turn round to return on the Weston-Sheffield (around 35 minutes for turning and watering) and was almost certainly rostered for a Peak. Engines noted were 44756 (55A) 6th July, 45564 *New South Wales* (55A) 13th July, 45268 (21A) 20th July, D99 (16C) 27th July, D86 (17A) 3rd August with 73156 (15E) on a relief, and thereafter Peaks worked this turn.

Westerns were few and far between but D1037 *Western Empress* (88A) did appear on 11.35 Weston-Paddington on 6th July and D1009 *Western Invader* (81A) on IM99 Penzance-Glasgow mail on 13th. A Weston-Wolverhampton extra provided work for a Stourbridge Grange on 3rd August this train crossing the Carmarthen-Weston hauled by 92236.

If these were the "highlights" of the season it can be seen that it could be described as "less than exciting". For the steam enthusiast perhaps the variety of Castles from London provided the most interest with two or three each Saturday with very few repeat performances. One of these locomotives returned to Bristol on the 17.56 ex-Weston stopping at all seven intermediate stations with a load of nine/ten coaches. 43 minutes were allocated for the twenty-mile trip. This train was sampled on 17th August with 7010 *Avondale Castle* at its head. Despite fairly sharp station work with stops of around thirty seconds except at Yatton and a maximum of 70mph between Flax Bourton and Parsons Street; a one minute late arrival was recorded in Bristol Temple Meads.

1964. In terms of diesel activity 1964 was more balanced with Hymek appearances reduced and most of the replacement power was in the shape of Westerns. Diagrams seemed to exist for locomotives from all the main WR depots for each of the classes except that the Old Oak Hymeks were not represented.

Only two regular steam diagrams remained

BRISTOL: Train IE68 standing where countless thousands of steam hauled services had done before. This view has since fundamentally changed with the construction of a "bridge" for use by the Post Office. Replacing the Standard Class 5 shown elsewhere in the 1963 view of the Weston-super-Mare - Sheffield service are English Electric Type 4 D369 and Peak D75. This must be an extremely rare pairing of these classes and probably unique at this location. English Electric Type 4s were never common in Bristol and were usually associated with excursion work. D369 had arrived in Bristol with a Coventry-Exeter relief. July 1966.   *(J. H. Sparkes)*

being 09.15 Bristol-Weston returning on 12.05 Weston-Sheffield and 13.07 Calne-Weston returning on 18.50 Weston-Swindon. These two workings however brought more variety than seen in previous years.

The Sheffield train power included 44805 (2E), 45280 (2E), 73038 (6G), 61153 (41D). 45557 *New Brunswick* (16F), D90(14B), 61093 (41D), 61051 (41D), 45060 (?) and 44805 (2E) through the season. The Calne working also had varied power although seemingly rostered for a Standard Cl.3 tank.

Recorded were 82038 (82E), 45407 (16F), 4916 *Crumlin Hall* (86C), 73073 (6G), 7928 *Wolf Hall* (85A), 82036 (82E), 82001 (82E), 82036, 82038 and 82001 again. As steam power was not rostered for passenger duties after the end of the Summer timetable it

seems probable therefore that 82001 hauled the last scheduled steam passenger train from Weston.

There were a few Brush Type 4 appearances with D1693/9 on Paddington services on 1st August, D1741 (11th July) and D1592 (4th July) on an unidentified South West-Manchester service.

The story for 1965 can be deduced from the earlier traffic surveys but the theme was clearly for the use of larger motive power of both Western and Brush types at the expense of Hymeks.

8.3 Excursion Traffic

Before we close the book on the Weston story a brief look at its excursion traffic, mainly at Bank Holiday time, provides some very interesting observations.

Weston used to receive large numbers of excursions being the nearest seaside resort to be reached from the industrial West Midlands or Paddington and the nearest in England when travelling from South Wales. On bank holiday Mondays large numbers of local visitors also poured in from the Bristol area. To accommodate these trains, every siding in the area would be cleared ahead of the bank holiday and an intensive steam shuttle, using borrowed large tanks from South Wales, would operate. In mid afternoon the "shed" at Weston which normally was host to two or three engines was surrounded by up to thirty visitors.

As dieselisation took hold the local trains first went over to Hymek and then DMU working until the road competition drastically reduced the need for these services.

Long distance excursions could run at any time between April and September and local enthusiasts were extremely dependent on the local "grape vine" for information on rare engines that were in town, especially mid week when "spotters" were supposed to be in school! News of the first Royal Scot visitor was greeted with great scepticism by those who failed to believe the messenger! A personal recollection was that of unrebuilt Patriot 45501 *St. Dunstans* (Rugby) on a cold Sunday afternoon in May (probably 1960).

The London Midland engines always attracted the most attention – these were usually Stanier Cl.5s but Jubilees also appeared quite often and Crabs were not unknown. More unusual ex GWR motive power was also seen with visitors from most depots East of Swansea which had a main line allocation.

Rare diesel power was provided by Peaks, Brush Type 4s (especially from the old WR Birmingham area), Westerns from Landore and Hymeks from Old Oak. A brief period of visits by what we would today describe as Cl.24s occurred as well as English Electric Type 4s.

Finally just a mention of D63XX – in case the reader thought these never reached Weston – during the Summer there was a regular Swindon-Weston duty which was used for running in ex-works locomotives. When new, pairs of D63XX worked through to Weston on this route, those in the D6330-40 range being specifically remembered.

SPECIMEN SATURDAY WINTER SERVICE SURVEYS
SURVEYS TAKEN AT SUMMER LANE, WESTON-SUPER-MARE
NOTES. ALL TIMES QUOTED AS PASSING TIMES FOR WORLE JUNCTION

ROUTES	UM – Up Main (Weston avoiding line)	UL – Up Loop (via Weston)
	DM – Down Main	DL – Down Loop

TABLE THIRTY THREE

Route	Loco	Shed	Time	Load	Reporting Number	Train	Notes
21st APRIL 1962							
A.M.							
UM	D845	83D	09.56	49	6D72		Freight
DL	D862	83D	10.03½	9	2B96	Bristol-Weston	5 Parcels
UL	DMU		10.21	3	3	Taunton-Bristol	82A
UL	D834	83A	10.40	9	1A42	Weston-Paddington	
UM	4968	82B	10.46	39			Freight
UM	5946	83C	10.51½	38			Freight
DL	D815	83D	10.55½	8	1B08	Paddington-Weston	
UL	D831	83A	11.07	12	IM91	Plymouth-Manchester	
UL	D7004	82A	11.15	30	9B00		Freight 1 Eastern Parcels vehicle
DM	D809	83D	11.18	10		Cardiff-Plymouth	
DL	6842	82B	11.39				LE
UM	2882	82B	11.38	18			9 tank Freight
UL	D863	83D	11.45	7	1A50	Weston-Paddington	
UL	D808	83D	12.06	8		Paignton-Bradford	Devonian
UL	6842	82B	12.19	7			ECS Midland stock
DL	DMU		12.32	3	2	Bristol-Taunton	82A
UL	D815	83D	12.40	8	1A64	Weston-Paddington	
DL	D805	83D	12.45½	9		Paddington-Weston	
P.M.							
UM	D1001	83D	14.10	8	1T30	Plymouth-Cardiff	
DL	D846	82D	14.19	47			Freight
DL	D855	83D	14.41½	7	1C79	Paddington-Taunton	
DM	D825	83A	14.55	13	1V93	Manchester-Plymouth	
UL	DMU		15.03½	3	A2	Taunton-Bristol	82A
DM	4985	83B	15.21	36			Freight
DL	DMU		15.30	3	A2	Bristol-Taunton	
UM	D847	83D	15.33	10	1H32	Penzance-Wolverhampton	Cornishman
DM	6965	83C	15.50	33			Freight
UM	D800	83D	15.55	5		Plymouth-Liverpool	
DL	D808	83D	16.31	11		Bradford-Paignton	Devonian 2 Eastern coaches
DL	D852	83D	16.45	8	1B15	Paddington-Weston	
DL	D847	83D	18.09	8	2B16	Bristol-Weston	2 suburban coaches
DL	D7011	82A	18.17	7	2C47	Bristol-Taunton	
DM	D1001	83D	18.20	11	1V95	Manchester-Plymouth	
UM	D601	83D	18.40	11		Penzance-Manchester	1 van
DL	D834	83A	18.45	8	1B19	Paddington-Weston	
UL	DMU		18.45	3	2	Taunton-Bristol	82A
UL	D834	83A	18.53		1A42		LE
UL	D847	83D	19.07	9	1A32	Weston-Paddington	1 van
UM	D816	83D	19.18	13	3C28		3 tanks, 3 vans. Parcels

TABLE THIRTY-FOUR

Route	Loco	Shed	Time	Load	Reporting Number	Train	Notes
20th OCTOBER 1962							
A.M.							
DM	D818	83D	10.07	12	3C16	Parcels	5 coaches
UM	D7050	82A	10.08	1	3H13	1 Brake	
DL	D7044	82A	10.11	5	2B96	Bristol-Weston	
UL	DMU		10.21½	3		Taunton-Weymouth	
UM	6320	86E	10.27	38		Freight	
UL	D856	83D	10.42	9	1A42	Weston-Paddington	
UL	D850	83D	10.51	11	IM91	Plymouth-Liverpool	
DL	D837	83A	11.01	9	1B02	Paddington-Weston	
DM	D7042	82A	11.05	28	6B83	Freight	
DL	DMU		11.25	3	2	Bristol-Weston	
UL	D7044	82A	11.46	6	1A50	Weston-Paddington	
DM	5071	82B	11.48	10		Cardiff-Plymouth	
UL	D830	83A	12.01½	9	1N37	Paignton-Bradford	Devonian
P.M.							
DM	D857	83D	14.41	13	1V93	Manchester-Plymouth	
DL	D842	83A	14.51	7	1C80	Paddington-Taunton	
UL	DMU		14.59	3	2	Taunton-Bristol	
DM	D7001	82A	15.10	50	6C21	Freight	
DL	DMU		15.25	3	2B53	Bristol-Taunton	
DM	D847	83A	15.39	11	1C41	Cardiff-Plymouth	

TABLE THIRTY-FIVE

Route	Loco	Shed	Time	Load	Reporting Number	Train	Notes
16th FEBRUARY 1963							
A.M.							
UL	6936	881	9.47$\frac{1}{2}$	5		Taunton-Paddington	
UM	6913	81D	10.05	38		Freight	
DL	D818	83D	10.20	5	2B96	Bristol-Weston	
UL	DMU		10.23	3	2	Taunton-Weymouth Tn.	
DL	6954	82B	10.34	30		Freight	
DM	D7040	82A	10.40	48	2B77	Freight	
UL	D801	83D	10.40$\frac{1}{2}$	9		Weston-Paddington	
DL	D831	83A	10.58	8	1A02	Paddington-Weston	
UM	D7052	82A	11.06	30	6T26	Freight	
UM	6833	84B	11.23$\frac{1}{2}$	53		Freight	
UL	6863	81D	11.33$\frac{1}{2}$	10		Plymouth-Glasgow	
DL	6981	82B	11.50	10		Cardiff-Plymouth	
UL	D818	83D	11.51	6	1A50	Weston-Paddington	
UL	D830	83A	12.03	9	1A37	Paignton-Bradford	Devonian
DL	3677	82E	12.06$\frac{1}{2}$	21		Freight	

TABLE THIRTY-SIX

Route	Loco	Shed	Time	Load	Reporting Number	Train	Notes
23rd FEBRUARY 1963							
A.M.							
DM	1000	82B	9.40	18		Parcels 7 vans	
UL	5908	82B	9.43	5		Taunton-Paddington	
UM	D855	83D	9.47	50	4B42	Freight	
DL	5056	81A	10.35	5		Bristol-Weston	
UL	DMU		10.35	4	2B	Taunton-Weymouth Town	1 van
UL	D852	83D	10.40	9	IA42	Weston--Paddington	
UL	D827	83A	10.51	10	IM91	Plymouth-Glasgow	
UM	D7050	82A	10.57	3	9B07	Brake & 2 Trucks	
DL	D842	83A	11.06	8	IB02	Paddington-Weston	
DM	D7044	82A	11.14	54	6C77	Freight	
UM	4972	82D	11.17	59		Freight	
UL	5056	81A	11.45	6		Weston-Paddington	
DL	6919	82D	11.48	9		Cardiff-Plymouth	
UL	D830	83A	12.01$\frac{1}{2}$	9	IN37	Paignton-Bradford	Devonian
UM	D7008	82A	12.11	58	F2	Freight	
P.M.							
DM	D809	83D	14.43	11		Manchester-Plymouth	
DL	D831	83A	14.47	6	1C80	Paddington-Taunton	
UL	DMU		15.01	3	2	Taunton-Bristol	
DL	DMU		15.23	4	2	Bristol-Taunton	1 van
DM	D855	83D	15.42	10	1C41	Cardiff-Plymouth	

TABLE THIRTY-SEVEN

Route	Loco	Shed	Time	Load	Reporting Number	Train	Notes

14th DECEMBER 1963

A.M.

Route	Loco	Shed	Time	Load	Reporting Number	Train	Notes
UL	DMU		09.24	3	B2	Weston-Bristol	
UL	D7020	82A	09.44	8	IA30	Taunton-Paddington	
UM	4703	81A	10.00	51		Freight	
UL	D7049	82A	10.04	22	099	Freight	
DL	D7007	82A	10.10$\frac{1}{2}$	10	5 54	Bristol-Weston	
UL	DMU		10.21	3	B2	Taunton-Weymouth	
UM	D7028	82A	10.26$\frac{1}{2}$	58	6B83	Freight	
DM	D855	84A	10.37	30	3C16	Parcels	
UL	D862	84A	10.39$\frac{1}{2}$	9	IA42	Weston-Paddington	
DL	DMU		11.03$\frac{1}{2}$	8	IC28	Cardiff-Plymouth	
UM	3822	86A	11.15	48		Freight	
UL	D7007	82A	11.45	6	2B9	Weston-Paddington	
UL	6878	82B	11.59			LE	
DM	D7025	82A	12.02$\frac{1}{2}$	15	6Z10	Parcels	
UL	D865	84A	12.06	9	IN37	Paignton-Bradford	
DM	6982	82B	12.09	38		Freight	

TABLE THIRTY-EIGHT

Route	Loco	Shed	Time	Load	Reporting Number	Train	Notes
21st NOVEMBER 1964							
DM	D1032	83A	09.44	48	6C35	08.50	Bristol West Depot-Hackney Freight
DL	D7097	84A	09.50¼	20	3C16	09.00	Bristol T.M.-Plymouth Parcels
UL	D842	83A	09.51½	6	1A26	09.40	Weston-Paddington
DM	D7014	82A	09.56	20	9B22		Freight
UL	D7024	82A	10.00		2B97		LE
DL	D7079	82A	10.04	5	2B96	09.35	Bristol-Weston
UL	DMU		10.23	3	2B	09.32	Taunton-Weymouth
UM	D866	84A	10.27½	45	8T71	02.50	Tavistock Jn.-Severn Tunnel Junction Freight
DL	9626	82E	10.30	13		07.58	Bristol West Depot-Weston Freight
DL	D7074	82A	10.51		2 97		LE
DL	DMU		10.52	7	2T11	07.55	Plymouth-Cardiff
DL	D7020	82A	10.57	9	IB04	07.45	Paddington-Weston
UL	D7074	82A	11.01			LE	
DL	D7029	86A	11.11	7	IC46	09.36	Cardiff-Plymouth
DM	D811	84A	11.25	53	6C38	10.45	West Depot-Tavistock Jn.
UM	D7014	82A	11.27½		9B03	LE	
UM	D858	84A	11.35	9	IM91	08.45	Plymouth-Liverpool
UL	{D7020 {D7079	82A 82A	11.41	9	IA40	11.35	Weston-Paddington
UL	9626	82E	11.45			12.05	Weston-Barrow Road LE
DL	D857	84A	11.50		Z34	LE	Reverse to DM 11.53
DM	D7099	84A	11.59	30	6C35	09.00	Severn Tunnel Junction-Hackney Freight

9. Diesel Substitutes

In the preceding chapters various parts of the story have shown that diesels were not always available to carry out their duties.

The introduction of the early diesel hydraulics did not bring about an immediate number of corresponding steam withdrawals. The Winter of 1962/63 showed that either by design failure or through lack of adequate precautions the hydraulics were not able to withstand extremely low temperatures although part of these problems lay with the train heating apparatus. In later years steam substitutes on passenger trains were far fewer – the substitute was another diesel taken from a freight duty, the freight train taking steam power instead.

Using official BR records an insight into what was really going on is now possible.

Diesel Availability

In the early part of the 1963/4 Winter timetable some typical figures on availability are as follows:

Date	Number Series / Class	Total Alloc.	No. Avail.	Avail. %	Rostered No. of Turns	Avail Reqd. %
27/9/63	D6XX/D8XX	76	51	67	60	79
	D1XXX	57	34	60	42	74
	D7XXX	86	67	78	68	79
6/10/63	D6XX/D8XX	76	59	78	60	79
	D1XXX	57	38	67	42	74
	D7XXX	86	67	78	68	79
16/10/63	D6XX/D8XX	76	52	68	58	76
	D1XXX	58	36	62	43	74
	D7XXX	87	69	79	70	80
25/10/63	D6XX/D8XX	76	54	71	58	76
	D1XXX	58	27	47	43	74
	D7XXX	87	73	84	70	80
2/11/63	D6XX/D8XX	76	51	67	58	76
	D1XXX	58	22	38	43	74
	D7XXX	87	66	76	70	80

In this period the examples show that in general Warships were in deficit on average four-six units whilst the Hymeks were almost on target for availability and, on one date, in surplus. The Westerns however showed deficits of between four and twenty-one.

By early 1964 an allocation of Brush Type 4s had arrived and are included in the data.

Date	Number Series / Class	Total Alloc.	No. Avail.	Avail. %	Rostered No. of Turns	Avail Reqd. %
10/2/64	D6XX/D8XX	76	45	59	60	79
	D1XXX	70	39	56	42	60
	D15XX*	18	14	78	10	56
	D70XX	101	74	73	72	71
14/2/64	D6XX/D8XX	76	48	63	60	79
	D1XXX	70	37	53	42	60
	D15XX*	18	13	72	10	56
	D70XX	101	79	78	72	71
21/2/64	D6XX/D8XX	76	50	66	60	79
	D1XXX	70	39	56	42	60
	D15XX*	18	16	89	10	56
	D70XX	101	85	84	72	71

The Hymeks showed a continuing trend of good availability especially on 21st February. The new Brush Type 4s* were also in surplus and although the Westerns were much nearer a low target figure it was the turn of the Warships to be well in deficit.

17th June 1964 presented a much brighter picture.

Number Series / Class	Total Alloc.	No. Avail.	Avail. %	Rostered No. of Turns	Avail Reqd. %
D6XX/D8XX	76	54	71	51	67
D10XX	74	46	62	50	68
D15XX	57	47	82	44	77
D70XX	101	75	74	83	82

Warships and Brush Type 4s were in surplus with a deficit of four Westerns (6%) on a higher percentage requirement (67%) and eight Hymeks (8%) although to plan for an "80% plus" availability was possibly ambitious.

Unfortunately further data is not to hand until August 1965. However this data covers all main line classes allocated to the region.

Date	Number Series Class	Total Alloc.	No. Avail.	Avail. %	Rostered No. of Turns	Avail Reqd. %
21/8/65	D1XX*	10	4	40	7	70
	D1XXX	74	52	70	49	66
	D15XX	141	107	73	118	84
	D6XX/D8XX	76	56	74	53	70
	D7XXX	101	86	85	77	76
	D68XX	168	155	92	138	82
	D63XX	58	49	84	47	81
	D95XX	49	39	80	37	75
13/11/65	D1XX*	9	2	22	6	67
	D1XXX	74	43	58	48	65
	D15XX	157	101	64	122	78
	D6XX/D8XX	76	48	63	55	72
	D7XXX	101	80	79	79	78
	D68XX	178	163	92	154	87
	D63XX	58	45	78	43	74
	D95XX	56	47	84	39	70

*The Peak Type 4s show a consistently poor availability whilst the smaller hydraulics have a good record. It is interesting to see the decrease in availability of D15XX after a period in service, this trend being continued in 1966 with consistent shortages of twenty units or more.

Had the 1964 performance of the D15XX been maintained compared to that of the Westerns a considerable saving in the number of units required could have been made. Even in 1965 the D15XX showed 6% better availability than D1XX.

To compensate for the lack of rostered power the operating authorities had only two choices – find an alternative locomotive (perhaps via a "filling-in" turn) or cancel the train. Surplus locomotives of a particular class of diesel might not however mean that one of these locomotives could necessarily be utilized as the surplus unit might for instance be at Landore with the turn to be covered at Plymouth.

At the end of this chapter some specimen

BRISTOL: Steam/diesel combinations were not too common in the Bristol area. This view was taken during the Winter service period and it is possible that Warship D860 *Victorious* only has the company of 5904 *Kelham Hall* to provide steam heating. The train is the 14.16 Plymouth-Manchester in the brief period when Warships worked through to Shrewsbury. 5904 has an eight-wheeled tender. *(J. H. Sparkes)*

day records of steam for diesel substitution are given. These extend outside the area covered by the traffic surveys as towards the end of steam on the Western Region it was the area around Worcester where most substitutions took place to keep areas where steam facilities had been withdrawn covered with diesel back-up for failures.

However there are many interesting and previously unpublished substitutions worthy of specific comment. It should not always be assumed that steam was failure proof – an entry for 11th October 1963 shows D1035 *Western Yeoman* substituted for Castle 7034 *Ince Castle* on a freight due to 'lack of steam'. None the less, D1035, itself was in need of attention within four hours on another freight working.

Two further interesting entries for 27/28 October 1963 are a total delay of 154 minutes to 22.36 Cambridge-Bristol freight which was hauled by D5669 – this must have been a very rare visitor to Bristol in 1963. The following note concerns 20.30 Paddington-Penzance which suffered an eighteen minute late start due to the key for the diesel being broken!

As noted earlier Westerns were frequently in short supply – a record sheet for 12th May 1964 lists all turns booked for these locomotives and shows the substitute situation. Firstly an extra Western was required as the Blue Pullman set was out of action and so a locomotive hauled set was required – D1002 *Western Explorer* was put on this turn.

05.30, 18.30 and 23.50 Paddington-Plymouth were worked by D824 *Highflyer,* D862 *Viking,* and D807 *Caradoc* respectively. 10.30 and 22.30 Paddington-Penzance had D822 *Hercules* and D824 10.45 Paddington-Weston, D836 *Powerful* with D808 *Centaur* on 12.30 to Kingswear. D836 was also involved in working 07.15 ex-Bristol and 16.33 ex-Weston services to Paddington. D870 *Zulu* was in charge of 16.00 Plymouth-Bristol whilst for Paddington services Plymouth provided D801 *Vanguard* for 00.30, D808 for 06.30, D862 *Viking* for 12.30 and D824 was in charge of 16.30.

Such was a typical day for this period.

Looking through the records of steam substitutions particular engines seem to be favoured, e.g. 4082 *Windsor Castle* in December 1963 on 10.40 Paddington-Plymouth on 7th whilst two days later it was in

action on the 21.25 Tavistock-Paddington freight.

It was not just WR locomotive types in trouble either – every day two-three substitutions were made on the Bristol-Birmingham route in 1963/4.

Britannia 70030 *William Wordsworth* was in use on 8th and 9th December 1963 firstly on 08.00 Wolverhampton-Paddington. Its return working is unrecorded though it was back in the North to take on 10.50 Crewe-Oxford (probably from Wolverhampton).

An interesting substitution on 2nd October at Reading was the station pilot – Manor 7817 *Garsington Manor* – which had to take over from D1068 *Western Reliance* which failed on a Shrewsbury-Paddington train.

30th October 1963 appeared to be a particularly bad day. The shortfall in hydraulics (particularly Westerns) was thirty-one. Nearly all the passenger train substitutions occurred on the Worcester and Wolverhampton routes to Paddington, the exceptions being two Gloucester-Swindon workings and a Paddington-Swansea turn where the steam substitute 5070 *Sir Daniel Gooch* was provided after three diesel substitutes failed. Twenty-three freight turns were also steam worked in place of diesels. 31st October saw thirty-eight passenger substitutions with 45572 *Eire* on 07.30 Shrewsbury-Paddington and 70017 *Arrow* on 10.50 Crewe-Oxford. The Crewe-Oxford turn was a favourite for Britannia substitutes with 70030/8 also being seen in 1963.

By the end of 1963 little steam substitution was generally taking place in the South West and yet there were exceptional days. 20th December saw 4079 *Pendennis Castle,* 4920 *Dumbleton Hall,* 5056 *Earl of Powis,* 5057 *Earl Waldegrave* and 7817 all active south of Taunton although only 7817 was on a class 1 train.

"Steam to the rescue" must have been the cry on 28th January 1964 when D7091 failed at Newport on 12.45 Cardiff-Manchester. Pannier Tank 3691 was the substitute working to Pontypool Road where D7038 took over.

Throughout the spring of 1964 there was continual activity of Castles on the Paddington-Worcester line. One entry shows 7029 *Clun Castle* on special "high speed trials " in January, these no doubt being in connection with the special train of 9th May from Paddington-Plymouth and return. As up to twelve Castles were specially prepared for this work it could be that some of the substitutions were perhaps more planned than the records show. It is interesting to note in this context that on 30th April (the nearest date for which records are available) eleven Castles were substituted for diesels on the Worcester line and yet not one of the select band chosen for the special duties appeared – no doubt they were all being fine-tuned and cleaned at this time. Also at this time Barrow Road Jubilees 45682 *Trafalgar*/45690 *Leander* were in almost daily use on the Birmingham route covering for Peaks.

Once the control of services on the former Southern Region line West of Salisbury passed to the Western Region substitutions were also recorded for that route and these ran at a level of four-five per day initially.

Friday 18th September 1964 – 70014 *Iron Duke* was recorded as working 01.10 Bristol-Sheffield passenger whilst 92220 *Evening Star* took 18.27 Llandudno-Old Oak in order to get it to Nine Elms for special duties.

6367 took a hand on a Paddington-Hereford turn on 22nd September following a Hymek failure at Pangbourne and in turn gave way to 6910 *Gossington Hall* from Oxford.

Another notable Britannia working was that of 70000 *Britannia* itself on 15.20 Cardiff-Gloucester on 5th January 1965 following the failure of D1719. It appeared again in the records on 21st September of the same year on 01.55 Crewe-Bristol and 11.53 return.

Stanier Cl.5 45050 found its way to Hereford on 28th September having taken over the 09.15 from Paddington at Oxford. It continued on the diagram with the 14.25 Hereford-Worcester and 23.15 Worcester-Acton freight.

About this time the number of LMS types reaching South Wales seems to have increased notably.

They appeared generally working WR based duties (from Cardiff and Margam) but seem to be the result of the outward locomotive – a Brush Type 4 being either failed or taken for other work. By this time there was virtually no Western Region steam left and the LMS types worked right through rather than being substituted by GWR types at Gloucester.

Thus it was that the real end of steam on the Western Region was courtesy of the LMS.

STEAM ENGINES WORKING VICE DIESELS
WEDNESDAY 9th OCTOBER 1963

DIESEL AVAILABILITY POSITION (4.00am WEDNESDAY, THURSDAY, 9th AND 10th OCTOBER)											
Class	Allocation	Booked Turns	Available		Exam		Factory		Repairs	
			Wed	Thur	Wed	Thur	Wed	Thur	Wed	Thur
8XX	76	60	58	54	4	4	6	6	8	12
1XXX	58	42	33	33	3	3	9	9	13	13
7XXX	86	68	69	67	4	5	4	3	9	11

Time	From	To	Engine	Reason
CLASS I TRAINS				
8.40am	Bristol	Sheffield	45690	Shortage of Sulzer Diesels due to maintenance & repairs
10.40am	Bristol	Newcastle	45653	D36 failed on incoming balance
11.00am	Plymouth	Manchester (X BTL)	5076	D815 failed
11.10am	Worcester	Paddington	7926	S.7035 on 8.0 HFD-WOS. No replacement
9.35am	Wolverhampton	Paddington	5031	D1008 used (stepped up), react to D1068 failed
8.35am	Salop	Wolverhampton	5070	Steam in balance. No replacement available
10.35am	Wolverhampton	Paddington	5070	Steam in balance. No replacement available
7.15pm	Paddington	Worcester	7926	Steam in balance (11.10 Worcester)
2.59pm	Gloucester	Swindon	5963	D6855 failed
3.50pm	Salop	Paddington	7923	D1039 failed. Steam to Wolv. D1006 forward
4.7pm	Reading	Trowbridge	6991	D7011 failed

TOTAL 11

Time	From	To	Engine	Reason
OTHER THAN CLASS "I" TRAINS				
9.00am	Bristol	Plymouth	6978	Diesel used to cover London service due to S.6963 on IX/ Plymouth-Bristol 8.10.
8.00am	Hereford	Worcester	7035	S.7035 on incoming balance
10.15am	S.T. Jct.	Weymouth	6972	D7013 failed (Electrical fault)
4.50pm	Margam	Swindon	6935	D1059 A.W.S. failure
5.20pm	St. Philip's	Water Orton	45447	Shortage of Sulzer Diesels
7.45pm	Kensington	Plymouth	5057	D817 used on 8.30 Paddn. vice D844 used on 3.45 Paddn. (D857 defective)
8.25pm	Southall	Salop	5031	Steam on incoming balance (10.00 Wolv.-Paddn.)
9.5pm	Acton	Margam	5256	D1045 failed @ 7.25. No replacement
5.00am	Gloucester	Hereford	6365	Pending trials of D7XXX on Ross-on-Wye branch
2.34am	Gloucester	Sheffield	45739	Steam in balance X NER (1.8 Leeds-Gloucester 8.10)
10.40pm	Old Oak Common	Bristol	6998	D7046 used on 10.20 Paddn./Hack. vice D7052 failed

TOTAL 11

STEAM VICE DIESEL IN LONDON (LOCAL) = 3
STEAM VICE DIESEL IN BRISTOL (LOCAL) = NIL
STEAM VICE DIESEL IN CARDIFF (LOCAL) = NIL
STEAM VICE DIESEL IN CORNWALL (LOCAL) = 1

TOTAL 4   **GRAND TOTAL 26**

STEAM ENGINES WORKING DIESEL TURNS
MONDAY 27th JANUARY 1964

DIESEL AVAILABILITY POSITION at 4.00am MONDAY, 27th JANUARY 1964						
Class	Allocation	Booked Turns	Available	Exam	Repairs	Factory
8XX	76	58	48	3	17	8
1XXX	68	42	40	3	15	10
15XX	15	9	12	–	3	–
7XXX	98	65	72	8	14	4

Time	From	To	Engine	Reason
CLASS I TRAINS				
11.15	Paddington	Worcester	S7029	No Hymek available (Six 00C Hymek under exam or in factory)
3.10	Worcester	Paddington	S7029	See 11.15am Paddington
7/15	Paddington	Hereford	5091	D7065 failed – no other Hymek available
8.40	Bristol	Sheffield	45685	Due Sulzer D1XX
12.05	Cardiff	Hereford	S6810	D7095 O/H Hereford for balance
5/50	Cardiff	Gloucester	S6845	D7037 failed
OTHER THAN CLASS 1 TRAINS				
10/40	Old Oak Common	Bristol	4919	D7065 off balance 6/40 Cheltenham. Sunday used on 3.25 Paddington
3.30	Taunton	Newton Abbot	7925	S7924 off balance 8.5 Tavistock Jct. Saturday
3.15	Tavistock Jct.	Taunton	4920	Laira unable to cover
10.05	Hackney	Tavistock Jct.	7925	See 3.30 Taunton
5.20	Bristol	Water Orton	73015	Due shortage of Sulzer D1XX
4.48	Bristol	Hunslet	45263	Steam Ex LMR
8.15	Bristol	Leeds	45682	Steam Ex LMR
3.45	Plymouth	Bristol	7925	Laira unable to cover
9.40	Tavistock Jct.	Taunton	4978	Laira unable to cover

TOTAL = 15

LONDON (LOCALS) = NIL

BRISTOL (LOCALS) = NIL

CORNWALL (LOCALS) = NIL

CARDIFF (LOCALS) = NIL

GRAND TOTAL = 15

STEAM ENGINES WORKING DIESEL TURNS
WEDNESDAY 12th FEBRUARY 1964

DIESEL AVAILABILITY POSITION (at 4.00am WEDNESDAY, 12th FEBRUARY 1964)						
Class	Allocation	Booked Turns	Available	Exam	Repairs	Factory
8XX	76	60	47	6	12	11
1XXX	70	42	40	2	16	12
15XX	18	10	13	4	1	—
7XXX	101	72	77	4	16	4

Time	From	To	Engine	Reason
CLASS I TRAINS				
8.53am	Taunton	Bristol	1010	Laira Turn, unable to cover
3.32pm	Bristol	Plymouth	6990	Laira Turn, unable to cover
1.15pm	Plymouth	Bristol Attached	4949	Laira unable to cover (D834 failed)
9.15am	Paddington	Worcester	6998	S.6869 in balance (10/0 WOS-PADN) owing failure D7062 at Woster. No spare Hymek
11.15am	Paddington	Worcester	7035	D7055 in balance used on driver training O.O.C. No spare Hymek
7.25am	Worcester	Paddington	7025	S.7928 in balance (11.40 PADDN.). No spare Hymek
11.10am	Worcester	Paddington	7005	S.7029 in balance (8.0 HFD.) No spare Hymek
11.15am	Paddington	Worcester	7035	No Hymek available
3.15pm	Paddington	Worcester	7032	S.7025 received on balance. No spare Hymek
7.15pm	Paddington	Hereford	7025	S.7005 received on balance. No spare Hymek
3.10pm	Worcester	Paddington	7011	S.6924 received on balance. No spare Hymek
11.10pm	Paddington	Worcester	5018	S.7011 received on balance. No spare Hymek
7.10pm	Worcester	Paddington	6998	S.7032 received on balance. No spare Hymek
8.40am	Bristol	Sheffield	45690	BTL Turn, unable to cover
		TOTAL 14		
OTHER THAN CLASS "I" TRAINS				
11.40pm	Paddington	Worcester	6974	S.6998 in balance. No spare Hymek
3.15am	Tavistock Jct.	Taunton	6963	Laira Turn, unable to cover
8.45am	Taunton	Hackney	6963	Laira Turn, unable to cover
12.05am	Tavistock Jct.	Taunton	1010	Laira Turn, unable to cover
4.30am	Tavistock Jct.	Avonmouth	4088	Laira Turn, unable to cover
1.55am	Taunton	Tavistock Jcn	5952	S.6918 in balance (9.40 TAVI.). LA Turn
8.00am	Hereford	Worcester	7029	S7029 in balance (7.15 PADDN.). 00C Turn
11.45am	Dr. Days	Old Oak Common	1010	D831 failed. No spare 8XX available
3.30pm	Exeter	Bristol	4949	D834 failed PLYM.&S. 4949 sent on 1.15 PLY.
3.50pm	Hackney	Bristol	6963	D7009 failed
6.50pm	Hackney	Acton	3854	D808 failed
2.0pm	Plymouth	Bristol Assist	5952	Laira turn, unable to cover
7.50pm	Avonmouth	Tavistock Jct.	5952	Laira Turn, unable to cover
5.20pm	S.P. Marsh	Water Orton	45186	BTL Turn, unable to cover
10.15pm	Bath G.Pk.	Derby	61143	DBY Turn, S.61143 received in balance (12.00 Lester BGP)
		TOTAL 15		
		GRAND TOTAL 29		

KEY

X BTL	Ex Bristol
HFD	Hereford
WOS	Worcester
Wolv.	Wolverhampton
IX	Inverness
ST Jct	Severn Tunnel Junction
Paddn	Paddington
TAVI	Tavistock Jct
PLYM	Plymouth
DBY	Derby
Lester	Leicester
Woster	Worcester

10. A Quarter of a Century on – and still Changing

The scene changes constantly, and quite often this is only really noticeable in hindsight.

Thirty years have passed since the traffic surveys were carried out and nearly every engine recorded has gone to that great locomotive graveyard. Perhaps in this respect many of the steam engines will have had a better end than their diesel counterparts, many of the numbers recorded forming part of today's preservation scene.

Moving on from 1965, the trend was for the increasing use of diesel electrics to work through to the West Country. Although little mention was made in this book of them, the D95XX 650hp hydraulics were on their way out not long after the steam that they replaced. Inroads into the ranks of the main line hydraulics started soon afterwards being replaced not only by Peaks and Brush Type 4s but also by Cl.50 locomotives transferred in from the West Coast route following electrification.

In 1971 the authors of *Summer Saturdays in the West* returned to do a comparative survey. It would have been a very brave man who in 1965 would have predicted that in a full day's observation of the Exeter-Taunton section only ten Warships and two Hymeks would be recorded. The Westerns at this time were still going strong and twenty-three members of the class were noted but the balance of power was in the hands of twenty-two Peaks and no fewer than thirty-seven Brush Type 4s.

"Foreign" motive power was no longer a Landore Hall or Penzance County but possibly an Immingham Brush (two were in fact

TAUNTON: The engines that ousted the Warships from many cross country duties were the Peaks. Class 46 46045 is seen departing from Taunton with a Newcastle-Penzance service on 19th April 1979. Steam had been gone for fifteen years but little had changed in this view apart from the train itself. *(Hugh Ballantyne)*

recorded). Other non-Western Region motive power came from Birmingham Division (8), Stoke Division (2), Nottingham Division (15), Gateshead (4) and Holbeck (5). Even Scottish examples were not unknown.

The advent of the HST removed the final Hydraulic influence before moving on to oust Peaks, Cl.50s and Brush Type 4s. Only the DMU soldiered on as it had done in years gone by and has only in the late 1980s/early 1990s been replaced by second generation build.

June observations at Taunton in 1974 by J. C. Hillmer showed that life could still be hectic with twelve trains in the period 12.00-13.00 and sixteen between 13.00 and 14.00. Observations began at 11.30 and continued until nearly 18.00. By this time Cl.50s had appeared on the scene and handled eight out of sixty-eight recorded movements, all apparently on Paddington line services.

Twelve Westerns were also employed with only two of the workings running to Bristol. With the exception of a Cl.31 and a handful of DMU turns the balance of services were in the hands of Classes 45, 46 and 47. It is interesting to note that five of the Cl.45s were still running with their original numbers, by 1975 only Westerns could be traced back by their numbers to 1965 surveys.

During the 1970s and 1980s Peter Tunks spent many hours recording movements at Exeter St. Davids. Although these observations fall outside of the geographical area of the book, all the data relates only to services which had passed through Taunton.

26th July 1975 found only subtle changes from the 1974 information. However the 12.35 Paignton-Birmingham service did produce a pair of Cl.31s and a single member of the class had a Barnstaple-Paddington working following a failure.

TAUNTON: "The Great Western Lives" – as much as could be allowed in 1984 with a lined green locomotive and brass name and number plates. Class 50 50007 *Sir Edward Elgar* has just passed Cogload Junction signal box (visible between the last coach and the power pole) with the 13.40 Paddington-Penzance. These services had seen everything through King, Warship, Western and Brush Type 4 before the arrival of the Class 50s which in due course would bow out to HSTs. 23rd October 1984.   *(Hugh Ballantyne)*

153

2nd August 1980 was the height of summer service operation and by then HSTs had arrived and over a twelve hour observation period covered some twenty Paddington-South West diagrams. The Westerns were long gone and even a Cl.50 had been ousted to work on the Bristol route. All the other main line work was handled by Classes 45, 46 and 47 again. A feature of the 1980 survey was the large amount of late running with many trains being 15.30 numbers behind time.

Six years later to the day (2nd August 1986) makes sad reading for the rail enthusiast with services reduced by some 20%. Quite drastic changes had also taken place on the motive power front. Now only HSTs, 47s and 50s could be seen. Paddington line services had either HSTs or Cl.50s in charge, the Cl.47s having been ousted from that route. HSTs now worked turns to Newcastle and Manchester, the Anglo Scottish trains being mainly in the hands of Cl.50s with Cl.47s on the balance of services.

And what of 1993? A survey carried out at Exeter St. Davids on the first Saturday of the summer timetable saw fifteen locomotive hauled workings but these included some on the Salisbury route. All these involved Brush Type 4s and these were the only link with times gone by except for a Class 08 shunter on a trip working. Two Class 37s and a Class 56

BRISTOL: The well known Western aspect of Bristol Temple Meads. Two holiday expresses are on view with the staple motive power that ruled from the early '70s to the mid '80s – Classes 45, 46 and 47. 47072 leaves at 11.30 with 6.38 ex-Leeds. 7th July 1979. *(Michael Mensing)*

were the only other locomotives noted. DMUs of Classes 150/2, 153 and 158 made up the balance with all other trains being formed of HST sets. Down locomotive workings on 17th July numbered just five – ex-Liverpool, Manchester, York and Glasgow to Paignton and a York-Plymouth.

The mature enthusiast mulled over his observations for the day at Bristol Temple Meads. His notebook was quite full of coaching stock numbers – two misformed DMUs and a clutch of HST queries and a renumbering being the high points. A reasonable number of locomotive numbers from Classes 37, 47 and 56 were to be found amongst the coaching stock along with a pair of departmental vehicles.

Then it was time to return to Weston. The Cl.158 glided to a halt, the automatic doors opening for him to board. The train was well filled but it was not necessary to rush for a window seat as once past Bath Road shed there would be nothing to put in the notebook – all the yards had long since emptied and freights no longer crammed the loops.

No longer would the traveller notice Flax Bourton or Puxton and Worle stations. These had long gone together with Yatton's two branches. The train would probably stop at the new station of Worle Parkway after passing under the M5 motorway. At Weston loop the train might have to wait for a Northbound train to clear the single line section from Weston.

As the train drew to a halt just under the new road bridge crossing the end of Weston station the enthusiast could see several road coaches and a mass of cars parked on the site of Locking Road station. With two way working in the station area the train had arrived at what used to be the up platform. The conductor guard had been through the train before arrival checking tickets and so there was no hold up as the enthusiast hurried

WESTON-SUPER-MARE: Weston-super-Mare in transition. This view was probably taken in the mid-1970s with Peak No. 14 approaching from Bristol with a train from the Midlands whilst Brush Type 4 1941 waits to depart with a Paddington service. The car and coach park to the right occupies the site of the former Locking Road station. The derelict area in the middle of the yard behind the Peak was occupied by a range of sidings, the goods yard and engine shed. In recent years this too has been taken over for car and coach parking. By this time hydraulic power at Weston would certainly have been a rarity.   (R. E. Toop)

through the tiled station entrance past the carpeted travel centre.

Ignoring the Mercedes minibus waiting for the few passengers who might need its services the enthusiast made straight for the car park, jumped into his Escort XR3i and made off into the gathering gloom, for home where the day's records would be studied and numbers checked off in the appropriate computer database.

WESTON-SUPER-MARE: The 'new look' Worle Junction. Outside the railway boundary housing estates have replaced open fields whilst inside the fence gone are an array of semaphore signals and the box to control them which stood in the now open space between the main line to the left and the loop line. The 'loop' also used to be double track, this now only remaining in the Weston station area. 43051 leads the 12.41 Weston-Paddington. 1st April 1978. *(Michael Mensing)*

WESTON-SUPER-MARE: Worle Parkway Station – December 1993. This view is taken from Summer Lane overbridge where the author spent hundreds of hours taking surveys in the early 1960s. At that time the bridge was surrounded by open countryside. Worle Parkway is served only by Regional Railways services. A previous station – Puxton & Worle – was situated some half a mile further North and was closed as a result of the Beeching axe. *(Author's Collection)*

The 12.30 service from Paddington to the South West approaches the Taunton stop. The headcode could suggest a locomotive substitution but if this is the case it must have been a fairly efficient move in view of the 135 minutes' running time assuming an "on time" departure from Paddington. D1003 *Western Pioneer.* 22nd June 1974. *(J. G. Hillmer)*

A Newquay service about to pass through the centre road at Taunton with 47232 in charge. In John Hillmer's survey in 1974 47027 headed this train. 6th September 1975. (*J. C. Hillmer*)

D1010 *Western Campaigner* heading a Penzance express passes a Class 50 at the head of a cross country service which has called to set down at Taunton. Behind the station sign on the left is the bay platform formerly used by arrivals from both Minehead and Ilfracombe. The centre island platform is now devoid of all buildings and except in cases of emergency is unused restricting operational flexibility. 6th September 1975. (*J. C. Hillmer*)

TABLE THIRTY-NINE

TAUNTON, 22ND JUNE 1974 SATURDAY

Down	45115	TO	11.35		IV63	
Down	1013	LA	11.45	9 coaches	IV46	Motorail Slough-Paignton
Down	47081	OC	11.38	10 coaches	IB18	
Down	1059	LA	11.53	12 coaches	IB25	
Up	1001	LA	12.00	9 coaches	IA59	
Down	47027	CF	12.02	9 coaches	IB95	Paddington-Newquay
Down	45112	TO	12.10	12 coaches	IV69	Birmingham-Paignton
Up	47157	CF	12.14		IE60	Through
Down	DMU	(C1)	12.19	4 car		Into No 1 Bay West
Up	47099	CF	12.22	11 coaches	IM85	Through
Down	57		12.25	12 coaches	IV70	Through to Penzance
Down	47042	TI	12.31	12 coaches	IB74	
Up	125	HO	12.32	Through	IE37	
Down	21	HO	12.38	13 coaches	IV71	Through to Penzance
Up	47033	LE	12.43	12 coaches	IA69	Through Plat. Penzance-Paddington
	(Loco green)					
Up	50050		12.48	9 coaches	IA75	Stop
Down	50030		13.00		IB35	Stop
Up	1557	CE	13.01		IM65	Through Newquay-Manchester
Up	1052	LA	13.06		IA79	Through
Down	26	HO	13.09	12 coaches	IV74	Stop
Down	47026	BS	13.11	14 coaches	IB39	inc. 2 sleepers. Through
Up	47191	CE	13.18	9 coaches	IM93	Stop
	(Loco green)					
Down	DMU		13.20			Arrived and reversed out at 13.25 and into 4 Bay (E)
Up	46051	BR	13.27	11 coaches	IM22	Through Penzance-Manchester
Down	46003	LA	13.29	13 coaches.	IV75	Stop. Crew change. To Paignton
Down	50048		13.32	12 coaches	IB45	*Cornish Riviera Express* Through
Up	50011		13.35	7 coaches.	IA05	Stop. Paignton-Paddington
Down	47478		13.43		IV76	Through
Up	47096	BR	13.44	10 coaches.	IM39	Stop. Penzance-Wolverhampton
Down	47254	HO	13.51	12 coaches.	IV42	Stop. Liverpool-Paignton
Up	45010	HO	13.53	12 coaches.	IM23	Through
Up	47089	OC	14.02	10 coaches.	IM28	Stop. To Birmingham
Up	46032	HO	14.10	13 coaches.	IE22	Through
Up	1063	LA	14.24		IA15	Through
Down	50007		14.27	13 coaches.	IB53	To Paignton
Down	47247	CF	14.30	12 coaches.	IV48	Manchester-Penzance
Up	45007	TO	14.33	13 coaches.	IE21	*Cornishman*
Up	1033	LA	14.42	11 coaches.	IA19	Crew change
Down	47331	TO	14.44	12 coaches.	IV77	Through. To Paignton
Down	1003	LA	14.46	11 coaches.	6S55	Stop. 12.30 ex-Paddington
Down	47493	BR	14.53	10 coaches.	IV01	10.25 Congleton-Paignton
Up	1011	LA	14.59	11 coaches.	IA3?	Paignton-Oxford
Up	47032	LR	15.10	10 coaches.	IM96	Stop. To Manchester
Down	45005	TO	15.12	12 coaches.	IV82	Stop. To Penzance
Up	47081	BS	15.17	10 coaches.	IC74	Stop. Paignton-Swansea

159

TABLE THIRTY-NINE (continued)

TAUNTON, 22ND JUNE 1974 SATURDAY

Up	50020		15.28	9 coaches.	IA?9	Stop. Paignton-Paddington
Down	47337	CE	15.35	11 coaches.	IV85	Stop. To Paignton
Down	50025		15.35			Through
Up	47453	CE	15.45			Through. Motorail
Down	46008	BR	15.45		IV86	Through. Paignton
Down	129	HO	15.58		IV87	Through To Paignton
Up	47231	CF	15.58		IM54	Through To Nottingham
Up	50009		16.18	13 coaches.	IA45	Through Penzance-Paddington
Down	46005	BR	16.32		4B10	Parcels
Up	31112	BR	16.38	8 coaches.	IA99	Barnstaple-Paddington
Up	45112	TO	16.44	13 coaches.	IM36	Through Paignton-Birmingham
Down	1006	LA	16.51	11 coaches.	IB73	Stop. Paddington-Paignton
Up	1034	LA	16.54	11coaches + 2 Motorail vans	04	Through
Up	27	HO	17.01	9 coaches.	IE73	Stop To Leeds
Down	1021	LA	17.03		8M53	Light
Up	DMU		17.08			Left E/Bay
Up	47491		17.08	9 coaches.	IA55	To Paddington
Down	DMU		17.18	4 car		Arrive.
Up	47502	BR	17.25	11 coaches.	IA65	To Paddington
Up	46050	HO	17.35	12 coaches.	IM29	Through Paignton
Down	47078	OC	17.38	12 coaches	IB83	Stop Paddington-Penzance
Up	1013	LA	17.48		IM61	Through Motorail

On stabling point. 31256 OC and a Cl.08.

Survey by
J. C. Hillmer

TABLE FORTY

UP TRAINS — EXETER. 2ND AUGUST 1980

Train		Loco	P.H. Time	Booked Time	Actual Time
06.26	Plym-Lvpl	45/46/47	07.29		
06.50	Plym-Padd		07.56		
07.22	Plym-Edin	47527	08.27/8	08.30	—/08.34
07.52	Paig-Padd	47471	08.37	08.37/9	08.36.5/8
08.05	Paig-Newc rlf	46013	——	08.51/4	08.50/3
06.05	Penz-Padd	43120/014	09.03	09.02/5	09.09/13
08.25	Paig-Sheff	45024	09.15/6	09.15/8	09.24/7
08.15	Plym-Leed	46019	09.22/4	09.22/6	09.30/4
08.45	Paig-Padd	47449	09.37/8	09.37/40	09.44/8
09.00	Paig-Newc	46055	——	10.00	10.01.5
09.18	Paig-Derb	47138	10.07/8	10.07/10	10.14/8
07.19	Penz-Padd	43009/008	10.13/4	10.13/6	10.21.5/4
09.35	Paig-Nott	45052	10.30/1	10.30/3	10.34/7
09.50	Paig-Lvpl	47035	10.42/3	10.42/5	10.45/9
10.05	Paig-Padd	50036	——	10.51	10.52
10.20	Paig-Manc	47187	——	11.02	11.07
08.24	Penz-Padd	43055/054	11.08	11.08/10	11.14/6
10.35	Paig-LD&HL	47220	11.26	11.26/8	11.33/41
07.57	Penz-Lvpl	46042	11.34/5	11.34/7	11.44/9
11.00	Penz-Brad	47060	—	11.46	11.52
09.00	Penz-Padd	43129/130	11.53	11.53/5	12.05/7
08.45	Newq-Manc	47445	——	12.09	12.15
11.20	Paig-Padd	50010	——	12.02/5	12.00/1
11.35	Paig-Manc	46028	12.26	12.26/8	12.27.5/34
09.15	Penz-Manc	46016	12.33/4	12.33/6	12.36.5/13.00.5
09.32	Penz-Wolv	50020	12.42/3	12.42/5	12.47/50
10.00	Penz-Padd	43142/141	12.53	12.53/5	12.54/9
12.10	Paig-Padd	50019	13.08	13.08/10	13.09/13
12.25	Paig-Nott	46031	13.18/9	13.18/21	13.21/30
10.00	Newq-Newc	45044	——	13.25/7	13.44.5/7
12.40	Paig-Birm	47147	13.31/2	13.31/4	13.34/41.5
10.36	Newq-Padd	47089	13.39/40	13.39/42	14.05/10
10.26	Penz-Brad	47497	——	13.49	14.14
11.08	Penz-Padd	43026/023	13.53	13.53/5	14.27/30
13.20	Paig-Padd	50006	14.08/9	14.08/11	14.22/4
10.53	Penz-Manc	47258	14.16/7	14.15/9	14.46/8
13.40	Paig-Oxfd	47480	14.30	14.30/2	14.38/9
14.00	Paig-Swan	47194	14.46/7	14.46/9	14.58/15.00
12.05	Penz-Padd	43035/034	14.56	14.56/8	15.13/7
14.20	Paig-Padd	47054	15.12/3	15.12/5	15.27/30
14.10	Plym-Bris	46033	15.37	15.36.5/9	15.49/50
12.14	Newq-Leed	46004	——	15.25	15.38
14.53	Paig-Sheff rlf	47029	——	15.43/5	15.54/6
14.45	Barn-Padd	25058/47293	15.41/8	15.41/50	15.57/16.13
15.05	Paig-Leed	45064	15.57/8	15.57/00	16.01/4
12.35	Penz-Card	46025	16.05/6	16.05/8	16.08/11
13.30	Penz-Padd	50025 a	16.13	16.13/5	16.31/3
15.35	Paig-Manc	46007	16.23	16.23/5	16.22/6
16.10	Paig-Padd	47109	16.59/00	16.59/02	16.57/00
14.02	Newq-Birm b	46001	17.16/7	17.16/9	17.18/23
14.00	Penz-Birm	50042	17.29/33	17.29/35	17.26/33
14.47	Penz-Padd	43004/005	17.49/50	17.49/52	17.49/53
15.37	Penz-Padd	43131/132	18.20	18.18/20	18.17/20
16.23	Penz-Padd	43039/038	19.23/4	19.23/6	19.29/32
15.58	Penz-Bris	45055	19.43/4	19.42.5/46.5	19.43/6

a: deputising for h.s.t.   b: extended to Sheffield

Survey by
Peter Tunks

TABLE FORTY-ONE

DOWN TRAINS — EXETER. 2ND AUGUST 1980

	Train	Loco	P.H. Time	Booked Time	Actual Time
06.35	Bris-Plym	??	08.10/6		
07.52	Bris-Penz	45055	09.08	09.07.5/10.05	08.53/09.09.5
07.25	Padd-Penz	**a** 43045/044	09.58	09.58.5/10.00.5	10.29/44
07.15	Oxford-Paig	47480	10.05/6	10.05/8	10.03/8
23.40	Edin-Plym	47097	10.15/6	10.15/8	10.11/6
07.30	Padd-Paig	50019	10.25/6	10.25/8	10.19/27
08.27	Card-Penz	47209	——	10.34	10.41
07.55	Worc-Paig	47147	10.43	10.43/5	10.55/9
08.25	Padd-Penz	43005/004	10.51	10.51/3	10.46/52
08.30	Padd-Paig	50006	11.29/30	11.29/32	11.24/30
07.28	Derb-Paig	45064	11.36/7	11.36/9	11.33/8
09.25	Padd-Penz	43132/131	11.45	11.45/7	11.42/6
08.00	Wolv-Penz	47098	11.56/7	11.56/9	11.49/58.5
09.30	Padd-Paig	47054	12.11	12.10.5/3	12.17/20
08.50	Swan-Paig	47194	12.20/1	12.20/3	12.25/9
09.25	Birm-Paig	46007	12.35	12.35/7	12.33/40
09.48	Padd-Barn	47293/25058	12.42/7	12.42/9	12.43/55
10.25	Padd-Penz	43038/039	——	12.48/51	12.46/9
08.58	Derb-Newq	47143	12.58/9	12.58/13.01	12.54/13.01
06.49	Brad-Penz	47477	——	13.07	13.11
10.27	Padd-Paig	47109	13.16/7	13.16/9	13.21/7
10.55	Padd-Newq	47159	13.34	13.33.5/6	13.36/6
11.25	Padd-Penz	43051/135	13.42	13.42/4	13.43/9
09.34	Leic-Paig	46018	13.51	13.50.5/3	13.53/8
08.39	Manc-Newq	47027	14.08/9	14.08/11	14.01/10
11.30	Padd-Paig	50021	14.15/6	14.15/8	14.12/6
08.40	Lvpl-Penz	50011	14.22/3	14.22/5	14.20/4
09.45	Nott-Paig	45037	14.30/1	14.30/3	14.30/3
08.36	Leed-Paig	45051	14.43/54	14.43/56	14.36/15.04
12.25	Padd-Penz	43014/120	14.49	14.49/51	14.43/15.02
09.35	Lvpl-Paig	47321	15.02	15.01.5/4	15.29/31.5
10.23	Manc-Penz	50001	15.12/3	15.12/5	15.47/50
12.30	Padd-Paig	50018	15.29/30	15.29/32	15.19/23
08.00	Newc-Newq	47459	——	15.21	15.39.5
13.25	Padd-Penz	43024/025	——	15.46/8	15.54/9
12.35	Birm-Paig	46048	15.37/8	15.37/40	16.02/5
10.40	Manc-Paig	47319	16.06	16.05.5/8	16.32/7
13.30	Padd-Paig	47562	16.13/4	16.13/6	16.39/46.5
10.14	Leed-Paig rlf	47487	——	15.55/8	16.17/20
09.50	Brad-Paig	47422	16.22/3	16.22/5	16.49/55
09.08	Newc-Paig	46051	16.30/1	16.30/3	16.58/17.01
14.25	Padd-Plym	47560	17.15/7	17.15/9	17.12/7
15.25	Padd-Penz	43017/016	17.45/5	17.45/7	17.33/45
12.23	Manc-Paig	45070	17.59/00	17.59/18.02	18.28/32
13.22	Lvpl-Plym	47147	18.44/5	18.44/7	18.43/7
16.25	Padd-Plym	43130/129	19.08	19.08.5/10.5	19.03/10
11.40	Newc-Paig	45001	19.17	19.17/9	19.14/7
09.50	Edin-Plym	47484	19.30/1	19.30/1	20.00/3
17.25	Padd-Penz	43141/142	19.49	19.49.5/51.5	19.41/50
14.32	Leed-Plym	95/96/47	20.37/8		

a: front power car defective

Survey by
Peter Tunks

162

2nd AUGUST 1980

OTHER OBSERVATIONS

Peter Tunks Records

	Train	Loco	Booked Time	Actual Time
06.10	Treherbert-Paignton Relief	47029	09.23/35	09.20/33
07.50	Kensington-St. Austell Motorail	50028	11.11	11.14
12.30	St. Austell-Crewe Motorail	47107	14.51/15.02	15.07
10.40	York-Newton Abbot Motorail	46056	16.43	17.23.5
15.00	Birmingham-Paignton Relief	47286	18.20/2	18.13/25
16.15	St. Austell-Kensington Motorail	50028	18.28/30	18.26
18.15	Paignton-Glasgow (IZ85)	45037	19.02/4	19.12/5

11. Appendix

Shed codes used

1962-63

2F	Woodford Halse
6G	Llandudno
8C	Speke
12B	Carlisle Appleby
14A	Cricklewood
14E	Bedford
15C	Kettering
16A	Nottingham
16D	Annesley
17A	Derby
17B	Burton-on-Trent
18A	Toton
21A	Saltley
24E	Blackpool
36A	Doncaster
41A	Sheffield Darnall
41C	Wath
41D	Canklow
41F	Mexborough
52A	Gateshead
55A	Leeds Holbeck
55H	Leeds Neville Hill
63A	Perth
67B	Hurlford
71G	Weymouth
72C	Yeovil
81A	Old Oak Common
81C	Southall
81D	Reading
81E	Didcot
81F	Oxford
82A	Bristol Bath Road
82B	Bristol St Philip's Marsh
82C	Swindon
82D	Westbury
82E	Bristol Barrow Road

WESTON-SUPER-MARE: Around twenty years and fifteen minutes later looking from under the clock in the first photograph – the signs have changed again and the 24 hour clock is the norm. The centre road has gone and HSTs reign supreme. 43152 leads set 253010 on the 13.14 Paignton-Paddington (via Bristol). 31st March 1982.
(Michael Mensing)

82F	Bath Green Park	5A	Crewe North
82G	Templecombe	5D	Stoke and Cockshuter
83A	Newton Abbot	6C	Cross Newydd
83B	Taunton	9D	Newton Heath
83C	Exeter	12A	Carlisle Kingmoor
83D	Plymouth Laira	14B	Cricklewood West
83G	Penzance	15A	Leicester Midland
84A	Wolverhampton Stafford Road	15C	Kettering
84B	Oxley	16C	Derby
84C	Banbury	16D	Nottingham
84E	Tyseley	41A	Sheffield Tinsley
84F	Stourbridge	41D	Canklow
85A	Worcester	41F	Mexborough
85B	Gloucester Horton Road	52A	Gateshead
85C	Gloucester Barnwood	55A	Leeds Holbeck
86A	Newport	70G	Weymouth
86C	Hereford	81A	Old Oak Common
86E	Severn Tunnel Junction	81D	Reading
86F	Aberbeeg	81E	Didcot
86G	Pontypool Road	81F	Oxford
87A	Neath	82A	Bristol Bath Road
87B	Duffryn Yard	82E	Bristol Barrow Road
87F	Llanelli	82F	Bath Green Park
88A	Cardiff Canton	83A	Newton Abbot
88J	Aberdare	83B	Taunton
88L	Cardiff East Dock	83D	Exmouth Junction
89A	Shrewsbury	84A	Plymouth Laira
89B	Oswestry	85A	Worcester
89C	Moeynlleth	85B	Gloucester Horton Road
		85D	Bromsgrove

1964-65

D14	London (Midland Division)	86A	Cardiff Canton
ML	Main Line	86B	Ebbw Junction
1A	Willesden	86E	Severn Tunnel Junction
1F	Rugby	87A	Neath
2A	Tyseley	87D	Swansea East Dock
2B	Oxley	87E	Swansea Landore
2D	Banbury	87F	Llanelli
2E	Saltley	85A	Cardiff East Dock
2F	Bescot	88J	Aberdare

Some other RCTS Books

BRITISH RAILWAYS STANDARD STEAM LOCOMOTIVES
Volume 1 Background to Standardisation and the Pacific Classes

Immediately British Railways was formed in January 1948, the Railway Executive instructed Robert Riddles to design a series of standard locomotive designs. The intention was to gain material savings in running and maintenance costs by adopting the best practices of the four independent companies.

In this major new series, the Society presents for the first time the complete story of British locomotive standardisation from the days of the Robinson ROD 2-8-0s to the twelve BR Standard designs totalling 999 locomotives. This book, by Paul Chancellor and Peter Gilbert, presents the Standards' design history and for each of the 66 locomotives in the popular Britannia, Duke and Clan classes, its complete construction, modification, allocation and operating history.

New larger page size, casebound, 184 pages, 151 illustrations including 17 in colour.

Locomotives of the LNER
Part 11 Supplementary Information

This mammoth series is the accredited expert work on the locomotives of the LNER. The first book in the series was published more than 30 years ago and since the publication date of each book much more new information has been discovered.

Part 11, the nineteenth and final part of the series presents the additional information with a relevant selection of previously unpublished photographs. An invaluable addition to the bookshelf of owners of other parts of the series.

Laminated cover, 98 pages, 85 illustrations.

RCTS LOCOMOTIVE HISTORIES
Great Northern Locomotive History
Locomotives of the LNER

The Society has produced the accredited expert works on locomotives of the GNR and LNER. Details of origin, construction, dimensions, rebuilding and withdrawal of each engine are presented together with sections covering detail variations, classification, engine diagrams and allocation and work. Photographs of each class and variations are included.

The GNR comprises four casebound books, the LNER nineteen laminated cover books. All the GNR books are available. Of the LNER titles, those currently in print are shown on our order form.

LMS LOCOMOTIVE NAMES
The Named Locomotives of the London, Midland and Scottish Railway and its Constituent Companies
By Rev John Goodman

The LNWR had a vigorous naming policy and the Midland Railway an equally determined anti-naming stance. The 1923 grouping set the stage for an absorbing battle within the management teams over naming policy with Derby's early policy success followed by Crewe's ultimate victory. This absorbing read presents the full story of the LMS and its constituent companies' naming policies and the history of each named engine owned by the LMS, a total of 812. The LNWR contributed 668 of these and a complete presentation of its complex re-naming system is an invaluable inclusion.
Casebound, 211 pages, 124 photographs, 25 drawings.

LMS LOCOMOTIVE DESIGN and CONSTRUCTION
Locomotive Engineers, their Designs and Modifications

Author Arthur Cook interviewed many LMS locomotive engineers over the years to extract much new material and give a new insight into their designs' origins and performances for this book. It initiates the main part of the Society's Locomotives of the LMS series, dealing with the post-grouping era.

The railway's design policies, origins and building programmes are meticulously traced with engine diagrams and modifications fully documented.

An account of the development of piston valves and valve events on the LMS includes an appendix outlining the fundamentals of valve events, invaluable for preservationists.
Board covers, 175 pages, 110 illustrations.

The Locomotive History of the South Eastern Railway

The South Eastern Railway route to the Channel Tunnel and ports is currently in the spotlight with its potential capacity constraint on international traffic. This book gives the complete history of the railway and its engines from their origins to withdrawal as late as BR days, including the important Cudworth and Stirling designs.
226 pages, 104 illustrations.

RCTS Publications list

*UK Post Free
Overseas add 25%

Title of Book		ISBN No.	*Price
BR Standard Steam Locomotives – Background **to Standardisation and the Pacifics**		0901115819	£19-95
LMS Locomotive Names		0901115797	£18-95
LMS Locomotive Design and Construction		0901115711	£16-95
Locomotives of the LNER:–			
Part 2B	**Tender Engines B1-B19**	0901115738	£13-95
Part 7	**Tank Engines A5-H2**	0901115134	£10-95
Part 9A	**Tank Engines L1-L19**	0901115401	£10-95
Part 9B	**Tank Engines Q1-Z5**	090111541X	£10-95
Part 10A	**Departmental Stock, Engine Sheds,** **Boiler and Tender Numbering**	0901115657	£10-95
Part 10B	**Railcars and Electrics**	0901115665	£13-95
Part 11	**Supplementary Information**	0901115800	£10-95
Gt. Northern Locomotive History:			
1	**1847-1866**	0901115614	£12-95
2	**1867-1895**	0901115746	£19-95
3A	**1896-1911**	090111569X	£19-95
3B	**1911-1923**	0901115703	£16-95
Highland Railway Locos 1855-1895		0901115649	£12-95
Highland Railway Locos 1895-1923		090111572X	£16-95
Shildon-Newport in Retrospect		0901115673	£10-95
Lord Carlisle's Railways		0901115436	£ 7-95
LOW STOCK TITLES – ORDER NOW WHILE STOCKS LAST			
Locos of the London, Chatham & Dover Railway		0901115479	£ 7-95
Locomotive History of the South Eastern Railway		0901115487	£ 9-90
Locomotives of the LNER:-			
Part 6B	**Tender Engines O1-P2**	0901115541	£10-95
Part 6C	**Tender Engines Q1-Y10**	090111555X	£10-95
LMS & GW Jt. Rlys Sectional Appendix to the **Working Timetables for 1933**		0905466845	£ 3-00
Locomotives of the GWR Part II Rail Motors		090111538X	£ 4-95

Available from:–
Hon. Assistant Publications Officer, Hazelhurst, Tiverton Road, Bampton, Devon EX16 9LJ.

When ordering please quote reference PUBS6

The Railway Correspondence and Travel Society was founded in 1928. Its objects are to help members in every way in the study of their hobby. A monthly magazine, *The Railway Observer*, is sent to each member. In addition, there are evening meetings at many centres throughout the country and visits to centres of railway interest. Members are offered discounts on new Society books.

Full details of the Society and how to become a member will gladly be supplied by Mr T. V. Edgington, 20 Baker Street, York, YO3 7AX on receipt of two second-class stamps.

LOCOMOTIVE HISTORIES

The Society has undertaken to publish a complete history of all locomotives owned by the post grouping railway companies. Details of origin, dimensions, construction, rebuilding and withdrawal of each engine, detail variations, classification, engine diagrams, allocations and work will all be described with illustrations.

The Great Western, London and North Eastern and Southern Railways have already been completed. Four books in the London, Midland and Scottish Railway Series have been published, and the first book in the BR Standard Locomotive Series.

Correspondence on, ideas for, and volunteers of help on publications are keenly sought by the Hon. Publications Manager, Mr A. R. Wood,